HOW TO

YOUR SERIOUS STEP-BY-STEP BLUEPRINT

WRITE

FOR CREATING INCREDIBLY, IRRESISTIBLY,

FUNNIER

SUCCESSFULLY HILARIOUS WRITING

How to Write Funnier

Book two of Your Serious, Step-By-Step Blueprint for Creating Incredibly, Irresistibly, Successfully Hilarious Writing

ISBN: 9781796818222

For the storytellers

Also by Scott Dikkers

How to Write Funny

How to Write Funniest

*Outrageous Marketing: The Story of The Onion
and How To Build a Powerful Brand with No Marketing Budget*

Welcome to the Future Which Is Mine

Trump's America: Buy This Book and Mexico Will Pay for It

43: A Portrait of My Knucklehead Brother Jeb (by George W. Bush)
with Peter Hilleren

E-Day! The Funniest Screenplay Never Produced
with Jay Rath

Our Dumb World
with the staff of *The Onion*

Destined For Destiny: The Unauthorized Autobiography of George W. Bush
with Peter Hilleren

The Onion's Finest News Reporting, Volume One
with the staff of *The Onion*

Our Dumb Century: 100 Years of Headlines From America's Finest News Source
with the staff of *The Onion*

You Are Worthless: Depressing Nuggets of Wisdom Sure to Ruin Your Day

*The Pretty Good Jim's Journal Treasury: The (Even More) Definitive Collection of Every
Published Cartoon*

Plebes: The Cartoon Guide for College Guys

I Finally Graduated from High School: The Sixth Collection of Jim's Journal Cartoons

I Feel Like a Grown-Up Now: The Fifth Jim's Journal Collection

I Got Married If You Can Believe That: The Fourth Collection of Jim's Journal Cartoons

I Made Some Brownies and They Were Pretty Good: The Third Jim's Journal Collection

I Got a Job and It Wasn't That Bad: The Second Collection of Jim's Journal Cartoons

I Went to College and It Was Okay: A Collection of Jim's Journal Cartoons

Commix
with Kathryn Rathke, Chris Ware, J. Keen, James Sturm, Jay Rath

BOOK **2**

HOW TO

YOUR SERIOUS STEP-BY-STEP BLUEPRINT

WRITE

FOR CREATING INCREDIBLY, IRRESISTIBLY,

FUNNIER

SUCCESSFULLY HILARIOUS WRITING

SCOTT DIKKERS

TABLE OF CONTENTS

Against the assault of laughter,
nothing can stand.

— MARK TWAIN

1

GET LEVERAGE

Simon Rich was fresh out of college with no professional experience when he sent a proposal for a book of short comedy pieces to an agent in New York. His book was so funny the agent leapt at the chance to represent him, and he had no problem landing a publisher.

That agent, Daniel Greenberg, called me to ask if I would read the book and possibly blurb it (that is, say something nice about it that they could print on the back cover). I read the book (*Ant Farm*) and, like Daniel, was blown away by its quality.

At the time I was taking a hiatus from *The Onion*, the humor publication I helped create, so I wasn't in a position to hire this undiscovered genius. If I had been, I would have hired him immediately. I called my friends at *The Onion* and told them about him, but they weren't in a position to hire anyone either. Not long after that, Lorne Michaels saw the book and immediately offered Rich a writing-staff position on *Saturday Night Live*.

After a nice run on *SNL*, he went on to work for Pixar and write several more books.

Not a bad career kick-off from one blind submission.

What was so great about Rich's work? How can someone captivate audiences so well with just some words on a page? Thousands of people write humor pieces every day of similar length, posting them on their blog, on websites like *McSweeney's*, or in the "Shouts & Murmurs" column in *The New Yorker*. Most submit their pieces to publishers only to get rejected. Why aren't all of these writers catapulting to the top echelons of the comedy world like Rich? What made him so special?

breakdown of all written comedy

funny   not funny

It's simple. His stories were really good. They were expertly crafted and sharply written. They were relatable, fun and engaging. Anyone who read them knew instantly that Rich possessed extraordinary skill, and had undoubtedly written his own ticket to whatever kind of career in the comedy business he could want. His pieces were short, smart, and laugh-out-loud funny. They gripped me from the start and didn't let go.

That's rare. A few written comedy pieces are *pretty* good. Some are mildly amusing. Most are not very good. To be honest, most are actually pretty bad. That's because writing short comedy prose and doing it well is an extremely difficult craft.

How did he do it?

Over the years, a lot of people have asked me the same question about my own work, and that of my staff of writers at *The Onion*. People—famous writers and comedy celebrities among them—wrote me kind letters marveling at the consistency of *The Onion*'s humor, admiring how original, insightful, and extraordinarily funny it was. They wondered if we had some kind of system or magic formula for churning out high-quality material on a regular basis. Like Rich, I was approached by New York literary agents and Hollywood talent agents. TV producers flew me to Los Angeles and chauffeured me around in limousines just for the opportunity to meet with me and convince me to work with them.

Everyone in the business recognizes quality humor writing when they see it. Such stark quality and competence is so rare, when it makes a surprise appearance, show-business executives jump out of their Eames chairs with starry-eyed excitement.

People who aren't in the business recognize it too. They might not realize how rare it is, and may not get as excited, but they appreciate it. More importantly, they laugh.

I know how Rich did it, and I know how others—including myself—do it too. Through trial and error, I figured out how to write short humor as owner and editor of *The Onion* on and off from 1988 to 2008. My staff and I wrote in a news-parody format, primarily, but we also wrote ad parodies, charts, lists, graphs, and first-person essays. And (once we started branching out into other media) some of us wrote radio and TV sketches as well. The positive accolades poured in. We won prestigious awards like the Thurber Prize in 1999, the Peabody in 2008, and more Webby Awards than we could count.

I recognized in Rich the same high standard and identical "best practices" for writing short comedy pieces I'd seen across media in all successful writing and in the writing I generated and oversaw at *The Onion*.

At the same time, countless writing submissions piled high in my inbox from hopeful writers. Their carefully written cover letters asked me to please consider publishing their work in *The Onion*. But none of these stories made the cut. Why? They just weren't funny.

The people at the top of the profession were doing it one way. The throngs of wannabes were doing it a different way.

GOOD COMEDY WRITING VERSUS BAD COMEDY WRITING

What makes some writing funny and other writing fall flat?

Like a lot of editors and comedy professionals, I know it when I see it. I can look at a great piece of writing and tell you exactly why it's working. More importantly, I can also look at a piece of writing that isn't working and tell you exactly what needs to be done to fix it.

Even though it's a learned skill, it's not subjective. It's not voodoo. It's a process. There's a playbook. And it works almost all the time. But since so much writing doesn't get laughs, and most comedy writers aren't achieving meteoric success, it's obvious that far too many people don't know this process, and have never seen the playbook. I've been writing and editing for so long that it's become second nature to me, and sometimes I forget that other people don't know how to do it.

That's why I wrote *How to Write Funny,* the first book in this series. And it's the same reason I'm writing *How to Write Funnier,* the follow-up.

But wait. Shouldn't I have told you everything you need to know about how to write hilarious, professional-caliber humor in *How to Write Funny*, the first book?

No. That was just the first part of the process, book one of the playbook. What I laid out in *How to Write Funny* was the single, foundational skill you need to learn before successfully writing a longer piece of humor. It explains how to create the essential building block of all humor writing: the one-line joke.

Every successful comedy writer has to learn this fundamental skill of writing jokes first. In the past, it was learned over many years of experimentation, bombing in comedy clubs, or angrily ripping up inept joke lists torn from legal pads. Only through dogged, foolish persistence were comedy hopefuls able to make any progress.

This method is, in fact, how I learned to write comedy.

In *How to Write Funny*, the secret of this fundamental skill is written down in a simple recipe you can follow. That recipe: compose a joke by formulating opinion-based Subtext and then passing that Subtext through one or more of 11 Funny Filters. This is the core skill of all humor writing.

Now, in *How To Write Funnier*, we're going to build on that knowledge, and turn one joke into a string of jokes that make sense as a unit. First you learned how to make an audience laugh once. Now you'll learn how to keep them laughing.

The road of a beginning writer is a lonely one. Most people who embark on the task of writing short comedy pieces do so in the silent vacuum of their own thoughts, hunched over a computer or notebook, constantly questioning their talent. They may work for days, weeks, or years, never showing their work to anyone. Some may engage a few confidants to give them feedback. Others might post a piece or two on a blog or maybe submit it to a publication. When such writers dream of big success, they imagine important decision-makers will magically discover their work and swoop in, plucking them out of obscurity to offer them the keys to the comedy kingdom like they did to Rich and me.

It might take years of agonizing hard work before anything like that happens to you. But with this book, I'll place helpful signs along the road for you. In other words, this book is your shortcut. Your leverage.

Instead of starting out blindly, flailing around discouraged, I want you to start out knowing the right way to do it. And then I want you to practice. And practice. And practice. By learning the playbook, you can adopt the right habits, the ones that will give you the best chance of success.

This book lays out the proper formula for high-level comedy pieces, the kind of pieces you see in "Shouts & Murmurs," *McSweeney's*, *The Onion*, or any other reputable magazine or website that publishes short works of humor. It's the same format you see on TV sketch shows like *SNL*, *Key & Peele*, *Tim and Eric Awesome Show, Great Job!*, *The State*, *Kids in the Hall*, *Mr. Show with Bob and David*, *Monty Python's Flying Circus*, and many others. I'm going to spell out in detail the skills you'll need to master the craft of writing these kinds of short comedy pieces, sketches, and scenes.

The good news is the formula is flexible. Your writing won't become "formulaic." Far from it. The steps you're about to learn allow you to be as fresh and original as you want, but force you to remain within the established framework and proper language of the genre.

There's never been more of a need for short, easily digestible humor writing. More TV networks, print and online publications, and entertainment media exists today than at any time in history, with more launching every day. And lately, people don't seem to have the time, attention spans, or desire to read for more than a few minutes.

Yet with so many outlets desperately needing content, it remains rare that a Simon Rich or an *Onion* comes along to dazzle everyone. The VIP pass to all the best distribution channels is still rarefied air.

I wrote this book to give you a leg-up on the competition. I'm passionate about good comedy, and by explaining how to do it the right way, I hope to inspire and motivate you to pursue your comedy dreams.

That's your leverage.

Let's get started.

CHAPTER 1 ACTION STEP

If you haven't done so recently, review How to Write Funny.

2

STICK TO THE PLAN

I've seen it more times than I can count. Editing *The Onion* and leading the "Writing with The Onion" program at the Second City in Chicago, I've seen beginners with no professional experience make their first attempt at writing comedy, and, like anyone trying something for the very first time (a musical instrument, a recipe, a dance move), they flop. Sometimes they feel as if they have a tin ear for jokes, and they wonder if they're a hopeless case. But after cocooning themselves and working through a deliberate process, they emerge like butterflies, creating their own hilarious comedy blogs, doing stand-up, publishing books, or getting hired to write for outlets like *The Onion*, Clickhole, Funny or Die, *SNL*, sitcoms, or movies.

The varied paths these people have taken to become successful comedy writers involve the same steps. If you want to achieve a similar goal, dodging landmines of disappointment and setback, all you have to do is follow their footsteps.

If you learn these steps, does that mean you have the same chance to enjoy the meteoric success of a comedy writer like Simon Rich? Maybe. It depends on whether you commit to doing the work.

Taking up comedy writing is no different than taking up any new hobby or sport. All the writers I've watched grow and succeed have practiced and practiced, writing piece after piece. They've followed the process spelled out in this book, they've walked the right path, and they've persisted.

Writing is a craft, not a natural talent. Anyone can learn it. And by saying this, I don't mean to diminish any of the masterful writers I've met and worked with in my career. To the contrary, I respect them tremendously for the time, effort and commitment they invested in building their skills.

If you dedicate yourself to the work at hand, practice, and remain open to improving, your writing will become more professional and you'll give yourself the best chance to succeed.

On the other hand, if you don't dedicate yourself to the work, and you rely on half-assed efforts, or believe you're already talented enough to succeed, get ready for disappointment. Success doesn't work that way. You have to pay your dues. And I'm going to tell you exactly what those dues are. If you don't pay them, you'll most likely remain an amateur.

FOCUS ON WRITING

The focus of this book is the short humor piece. You can call it an article, a story, or whatever you want. I'll use the term "piece" throughout the book, referring to prose beyond the length of a single joke. This is any type of humorous writing that's at least a paragraph, but no longer than a couple of pages of typed prose and no more than five or six pages in typed script format. In this genre of writing, a single concept is extrapolated into long-form prose using comedic structure. A short humor piece can be an article, song, essay, list, listicle, ad parody, poem, sketch, stand-up bit or rant. For the purposes of this book, I'll be focusing on the prose medium. Why? Composing a prose piece requires much more discipline than writing in other media. If your focus is sketch comedy or stand-up,

I recommend you follow this process and learn to write prose. By learning to write a tight prose piece, your sketch and stand-up writing will dramatically improve.

FUNNIER-WRITING TIP #1: THERE'S NO SUCH THING AS TALENT

Do you think Steve Martin bought a typewriter one day and immediately wrote The Jerk? *What makes success? Hard work, persistence, and skill development. People who focus on these three things, like Martin, improve their work and are the ones who get good, who become "great talents." Don't fall for the myth that you need talent to succeed. If you find your inner voice saying, "I just don't have the talent to achieve this," realize that's just another way of saying "I'm not willing to do the work necessary to achieve this," because that is, in fact, what you're really saying. Commit yourself to the work and you'll become talented.*

A "story," on the other hand, is another beast entirely. I use the term "story" to define any work of writing—including humor writing—that uses dramatic structure. This is storytelling. Even though it might reside squarely in the humor genre, a story of any length—even a single line— uses dramatic structure. We'll delve deeper into the difference between comedic and dramatic structure (and why this distinction is important) in chapter 16. For now we'll focus on comedy structure.

Follow the action steps at the end of each chapter for the step-by-step process a writer goes through to write a single work of prose comedy. In chapter 14, you'll find samples of several written pieces, from rough draft to published draft, that have gone through the same process. You'll learn how to stay on track and avoid typical pitfalls.

Upon completing the action steps in this book, practice by repeating them with another piece, and then another. Stick with it and soon you'll be perfecting your ability to create a funny piece of writing.

If you haven't read book one, *How to Write Funny,* please stop reading and go do that now. You need to be competent at writing a single-line joke before you can expect to string several jokes together into a humorous article, essay, or story, building on each joke to escalate the humor. The concepts and terms I introduced in *How to Write Funny* will be referenced in this book repeatedly, and will sound like gobbledygook to the uninitiated.

If you choose to ignore me and skip *How to Write Funny*, you'll probably find this book challenging and confusing. For example, if you suffer from writer's block, or repeatedly ask yourself, "How do I come up with ideas?" you're experiencing basic problems that are thoroughly addressed in *How to Write Funny*. If that's where you are, start with that book.

Furthermore, the foundation you need in order to start writing comedy doesn't come from just reading a book. Read and familiarize yourself with the concepts in *How to Write Funny*, but do the exercises too. Get good at writing jokes first. *How to Write Funny* can get you there.

As for this book, I recommend reading it front to back, without jumping around. If you're serious about learning the craft of comedy, read it through without taking notes and do the exercises. Then read it through again, take notes, and do the exercises again. After that, you'll grow confident with the process, and you can keep the book handy as a reference guide.

OVERVIEW

The process of writing short comedy pieces begins with a joke. But to get one joke, you need dozens—sometimes hundreds—of jokes. If you did the action steps in *How to Write Funny*, you should now be in possession of plenty of jokes for this purpose. (Look for more tips on how to generate jokes in the next chapter.) One of these jokes will serve as the title of your written piece. A comedy piece requires a funny title for two reasons:

First, you need to communicate the genre to your audience. If you present readers with a big block of copy without any clue as to what kind of writing it is, or what the writing is about, they won't read it. No one in this day and age will start reading unidentified copy at random, hoping it's something they're interested in. They need to know whether they want to read it. A title must also clearly and succinctly communicate the tone and concept of your writing so readers know in advance what your writing is about. The quality of your title is especially important with humor; a funny title communicates, "This is a humor piece." However, if your title tries to be funny and fails, people may realize it's a humor piece, but they'll assume it isn't funny, and they won't read it.

the SIX steps to mastering comedy writing

1. practice
2. practice
3. practice
4. practice
5. practice
6. practice

Second, your title plants a comedy seed. Readers are intrigued when they read a funny title. They like your joke and want to see it expanded.

Once you have a big pile of titles, the important process of weeding through them begins. Using all the criteria you learned in *How to Write Funny*, you'll determine which ones work best. You'll go through all the tips and best practices for joke writing to vet your ideas; you'll omit needless words, make sure they're not too complicated, make sure the funny part comes last, etc.

You'll get other people to review your ideas and chime in. Detailed tips for this part of the process are in chapter 5.

Armed with this new feedback, you'll select the funniest idea from the pile and put it on a separate list. This list contains your ideas that are the most bankably funny, and are intriguing enough to hold the reader's attention beyond a single line.

While making your list, other ideas may spring forth, such as ideas for bigger projects, stand-alone jokes, a great concept for a novel, etc. Save these ideas! Organize them on separate lists and compile all similar ideas into their own lists: make a list for TV show ideas, movie plots, website ideas, etc. For our purposes, we'll focus on one list: your best ideas for short comedy pieces.

To get started, you'll pick one idea. More criteria for selecting a winning title can be found in chapter 4.

Once you've selected the idea, you'll make a bullet-point list of additional jokes stemming from your core concept. You'll want a list of at least 20 additional jokes that flesh out the comedy world of your joke. You'll do this on your own, or for better results, enlist the help of others. Tips for doing this are in chapter 9.

Next, you'll hammer out a bad rough draft by stringing together the jokes you riffed, then filling in the connective material. The sole focus of your first draft is quantity, not quality. Write something, anything. Sounds easy, but it's a big hurdle for many new writers. I'll walk you through it in chapter 11.

When you have a bad rough draft, you'll let it sit for a while, forget about it, and then come back to it later with fresh eyes. This will give you a valuable sense of objectivity, like you're a reader who just happened upon your piece. You'll set yourself up to be honest about it, asking if the piece lives up to the potential suggested by its title. Then you'll rewrite your piece, improve it, simplify it, and make sure it has "joke discipline" (chapter 9). You'll show this rewritten draft to people who can give you critical feedback, then you'll take their feedback to heart and rewrite your piece again. (Ways to survive the challenges of a second draft are covered in chapter 13.) You'll then rewrite your piece again until it feels funny enough to show to a wider audience.

Getting useful feedback on jokes is tricky. Getting useful feedback on a competed piece of comedy is even trickier. Knowing what notes to act on and which ones to ignore is difficult. It takes experience to know how to balance the opinions of others with your own inherent sense of what's working. In chapters 13 and 15 I'll give you tools to work through this potential quagmire so the best decisions to improve your writing come quickly.

After these steps, you'll have a completed comedy piece that has a fighting chance to get laughs.

CHAPTER 2 ACTION STEPS

1. Collect any short jokes you've already written to serve as titles of a longer written piece.

2. Begin reading professional short humor pieces. Analyze them and see if you can find similarities. You'll begin to see the established structure of all short written comedy that will be described in the next few chapters.

3

MAKE REGULAR DEPOSITS

If you don't already have a 401K retirement account, someone has probably recommended you open one. Building some financial security in your future is the wise and responsible thing to do. The idea of a 401K account is that you consistently squirrel a little money away during your working life to ensure your living expenses are covered when you retire.

I recommend you create that same sense of security for your joke writing. Start making deposits into the 401K plan of your comedy career. Just like putting a little money away every day is smart, putting a little comedy away every day is a good idea too.

When you save consistently in a stock-based retirement plan, you use the investment technique known as "dollar cost averaging." Translation: Buy stocks when the market is down, but also buy stocks when the market is up. Investing this way evens out your risk. The same rule applies when you consistently write funny ideas, every day, no matter how you're feeling. You'll make deposits when you're on fire and feel like every idea is golden, and you'll make deposits when you feel like every idea is terrible.

Save every joke like it's as valuable as money. Keep them somewhere safe, and if that place is your computer, back up your lists in the Cloud or on an external drive so you don't lose them.

Cultivate this habit by spending about 20–30 minutes every day coming up with new jokes. The more days you do this, the stronger your comedy writing foundation. If you don't feel like you have time to do this, try spreading out the task, generating a few jokes while you're showering, waiting in line at the grocery store, or stuck in traffic. By multitasking in this way, you'll make the most productive use of your time.

Anyone who's serious about improving their comedy writing skills needs to actually write comedy, and one of the best ways to write comedy is to write 10 jokes every day.

By "joke," I mean one short line that's funny, potentially funny, or even just trying to be funny. I also mean any idea for a comedy project: a book, a movie plot, a cartoon. Here are some sample jokes from such a list (I'm just writing these off the top of my head), so you can get an idea of what a typical joke list might look like:

1. *You should leverage what you're best at to start a business. How can I leverage napping?*
2. *A man hanging up a picture can't seem to get it to hang straight no matter how many times he tries.*
3. *Someone tells their life story in a pictogram.*
4. *A rebus breakup note.*
5. *Firing someone via emojis.*
6. *An electric fan fights valiantly against an oppressive heat wave using the only weapon it has: the ability to blow air around.*

7. *The president should not allow people in white clothes to come into the White House because what if they blend in and look like floating heads? The president is too important to be dealing with that.*

8. *Story about the Washington DC janitor who lives at the top of the Washington monument.*

9. *Sociopath Media*

10. *Intelligent life is discovered on a nearby planet, and a loser is selected by the UN to be sent to this planet to be the sole representative of all humanity.*

As you can see, many of these ideas aren't great. But a list of 10 ideas written in 20–30 minutes is rarely going to be great. That's okay. The important thing to remember is that you're creating a daily habit of writing ideas. Every once in a while you'll have a good one. For those, the effort is worthwhile.

The rationale behind writing these ideas every day is to give you the quantity of ideas necessary to achieve quality. In order to write a funny piece of comedy, you need a winning concept, and the best way to come up with one winning concept is to write dozens of concepts, and then chose only the best one from among the chaff. You need raw material to find gems.

Assuming about 90 percent of everything you write is garbage (a realization made famous by sci-fi author Theodore Sturgeon), for every list of 10 ideas, you might have one worthy of expanding into a longer piece of writing.

By writing 10 ideas every day, you'll start to compile an impressive backlog. In time, you'll never be at a loss for something to write about.

The most common struggles for wanna-be comedy writers are that they don't know what to write about, don't have any ideas, or lack the discipline to even try. This daily habit solves all three of these problems.

Comedy writers who don't commit to writing a lot of ideas have an extremely difficult time succeeding. They often have one idea they're especially in love with, then go through life will all their hopes and dreams pinned to it. If anyone tries to give them feedback on their one idea, their spirit will likely be crushed. When so much of a writer's future is invested in one idea, it's almost impossible not to take criticism personally. The chances of a writer like this succeeding with their one idea are miniscule.

In relationships, they call this "one-itis," and the symptoms are the same. The writer has fallen hard for this one idea and believes it's the best and only idea that will ever come to them, therefore they must invest everything they have in it. Beyond that, they spend far too much time writing it and rewriting it, trying to "perfect" it before showing it to the world. Ultimately, such an idea, and the humor writing that springs from it, is worthless. The writer is too attached to make any meaningful improvements or branch out and try something else that might challenge them.

Professional comedy writers have tons of ideas, and when they get feedback to help them chose which ideas are best, they coldly discard the ideas that don't work and save the ones that do.

FUNNIER-WRITING TIP #2: BE ORIGINAL

Be no less diligent about eradicating clichés in your longer-form comedy than you are in your one-line jokes. Clichés are a cancer in humor writing. Clichéd jokes, topics, phrases, or scenarios—anything that's too similar to something that's come before it—can doom a work of comedy. Fresh and original writing delights the biggest and broadest possible audience.

Every month, go through your lists and organize them. If you have some peers to give you feedback, accept it. Trash the ideas that are hopeless. Save the good ones on a short list. Put the movie ideas on a separate list, the sketch ideas on another, and the jokes on another. Title each list accordingly.

Organizing your ideas onto separate lists turns your comedy output into an easily accessible savings account. It prepares you to respond when given the opportunity to submit ideas to a publication or show. Such opportunities usually come without warning and with a fast-approaching deadline. Often, a comedy writing colleague will know someone who knows someone, and they'll announce that this show or that publication is hiring. These lists put you in an excellent position to quickly compile material, giving you a much better chance to take advantage of any opportunity.

joke   short comedy
                                  piece

Maybe you meet someone who works for a movie studio at an industry party and they mention they're looking for comedy scripts about the Olympics. Or you meet someone at a comedy club who works for *Mad* magazine and they mention they're eager to buy funny listicles about the U.S. Congress. By scanning your various lists, following up with a pre-vetted and on-topic inquiry or submission is easy. Whenever you need a funny idea, instead of trying to come up with one off the top of your head, which almost guarantees it will be weak, go to your exhaustive file of ideas and find one that's just right for the occasion. Don't rely on desperate, last-minute work. By Sturgeon's Law, you'd need to come up with ten ideas off the top of your head to have any chance of coming up with a good one. Professional writers have ideas in the bank. And when opportunity presents itself, they make a withdrawal.

Better yet, if you have designs on one day working for a certain TV show or comedy publication, focus your ideas on the style of that TV show or publication. Compile a list of jokes or sketch ideas over time especially for that outlet. With this kind of targeted effort, you won't even have to write a submission packet if opportunity suddenly and unexpectedly knocks. You'll merely pull your completed packet from your file, format it a little bit, maybe add a couple of timely jokes, and then send it right over. They'll be impressed by how fast you produced it.

If you're focused less on getting a job writing comedy for someone else and more on creating comedy for your own brand, a deep well of ideas is even more valuable. You'll draw on a list of ideas for consistent output, selecting only the best ideas to execute as longer-form pieces for your comedy blog, stand-up routine, or YouTube channel. And you can be assured your material will be higher quality than if you had just executed the first idea that came into your head.

CHAPTER 3 ACTION STEP

Write at least 10 funny jokes or concepts every day. Make this a daily habit, spending no more than 30 minutes on it. Writing these daily jokes will give you a wealth of raw comedy material to expand into comedy pieces, stories, articles, sketches, or stand-up bits.

4

CHOOSE WISELY

Years ago, short comedy pieces were written differently than now. They were written something like this: a funny writer hammered it out, then an editor or head writer would give it a pass, maybe ask for some changes, then a title would get slapped on it, then a designer would lay it out, and then it would get published. Sometimes it was funny, but more often than not the audience was confused. They'd ask, "What's the story about?" "Why should I read it?"

But it didn't matter. Readers had nowhere else to go. If they wanted to read humor, their only choice was one of two established channels that offered funny writing: (1) books from major publishers and (2) national magazines. Short sketches using the same format also appeared on stage and in sketch TV shows, but in terms of the written word, it was a desert out there.

These books and magazines were recognized brands. It was nearly impossible to break through their monopoly and reach readers if you weren't already in their exclusive club. And almost no one knew how to break into it.

Thankfully, this situation has radically transformed, in two major ways. First, there are countless new outlets that publish or present short comedy, and many of them are far more accessible than any in the past. Anyone can publish their work online. Staff writers for well-known comedy brands are on Twitter and you can ask them questions directly. You can Google "How to Submit to XYZ publication" and find answers from a number of different sources.

But it's the second way things are different that I want to focus on. Did you notice the step in the middle of the old process, "a title would get slapped on it." This critical link in the chain used to be an afterthought. And it made sense that it was. When books and magazines didn't have any competition, they didn't have to work very hard to compel readers to read their humor. *The New Yorker* (with its "Shouts & Murmurs" column) and *The Harvard Lampoon* may be the only publications that still do things this way. *The New Yorker* doesn't need to entice anyone to read the "Shouts & Murmurs" column. They already have millions of readers who all know what to expect from it: a wry, amusing, well-written story in the humor genre. *The Harvard Lampoon* isn't competing for ad dollars or space on newsstands. They're supported by an endowment and operate as a student project.

But everywhere else—and I don't just mean other humor publications like *Mad*, *The Onion* and others, I mean the overwhelming majority of outlets offering short comedy—there is a fevered and desperate effort to grab the reader's attention. Especially among those without a platform or name recognition, simply presenting stories with no thought to the title is a blueprint for failure. Just about everyone is in the trenches fighting for eyeballs. The lucky few who can grab your attention and keep it might even be able to scratch out a living and, over time, do well. Those who can't are doomed.

In the age of the Internet and the Attention Economy, you're fighting to somehow compel readers not only to discover your work but actually invest the time necessary to read it. That's a lot to ask. Your title is your best chance to wow them because it's the first thing they'll see. It needs to promise a reading experience that will leave them in stitches. Miss that chance, and you'll likely never get another.

FUNNIER-WRITING TIP #3: REMEMBER THE FIRST LAUGH

When selecting the one idea to expand into a piece of writing, boredom may set in after you've thought about it for a time. You may get even more bored once you start working on the first lines of the piece. Your writing will start to veer into crazy new directions in order to jazz up what you now find to be a thoroughly boring idea. Or, you may give up on writing the piece altogether because you've decided the idea is just not funny anymore. When this happens, remember how funny it was when you first thought of it. Remember the laughs it got when you first ran it by someone whose judgement you respect. Those initial reactions are the only ones that matter. Readers won't get bored with your idea because they won't live with it for hours like you will. They'll spend a few seconds reading it and, if you've done your job well, laughing at it. It's natural for you, the creator, to forget this extremely brief reader experience and overthink your joke. Don't! Those few seconds are everything to you. They're a portal to a universe of success that only opens for a split second. Stay focused, and don't lose sight of the original appeal of your idea. If you do, you'll miss your chance to jump through the portal.

A particular image, enlarged text at the top of your story, or a myriad other layout tricks might further entice readers to give your writing a try, but you may not have any control, ultimately, over the layout or contextualization of your writing. The design and how pull-quotes or images are used will depend on where it's presented. Your title, then, remains the best, most important tool you have to exercise any measure of control over a reader's behavior. A funny title is what you need to get clicks.

Your title is a beacon to the world, signaling, "Hello out there! I have something you might find funny! Come here and take a look at it! Try the first few lines at least!"

A title is your one chance to grab attention, so it can't be a dud. Chose the best title in your arsenal and write a comedy piece based on it. Writing a funny piece and then trying to think of a funny title for it afterwards doesn't work. That's like trying to put a scrambled egg back together. It's far more efficient to come up with a winning concept before investing any precious time writing it up.

SELECTING A WINNING IDEA

After doing the Action Steps in *How to Write Funny*, you should be sitting on a big list of concepts, titles, and short jokes. If you've already started writing 10 jokes a day as I advised in the last chapter, you'll have a few more. That's exactly where you want to be. Now you can chose one of them. Leave emotion out of this process. Rely on intellect. Put your editor hat on and be honest with yourself. If you love an idea, especially if it's your only idea, do not immediately select that idea.

Get your master list of jokes in hand, go through each one, and judge them one by one using the following Title Approval Gauntlet:

1. The joke has good Subtext.

You want to make sure your joke has something to say—a worthy thing to say. It doesn't have to be earthshakingly brilliant, but it has to be something. And you have to be aware of what it's saying in order to articulate it subtextually. If the joke has interesting Subtext, advance to number 2. If it doesn't, reject it.

2. The joke uses one or more Funny Filters.

Your joke must employ at least one, and ideally more than one, Funny Filter, used properly. If it does, advance the joke to number three. If it doesn't, reject it.

3. The joke employs the best practices of a funny one-liner.

Make sure the joke adheres to the Funny-Writing Tips sprinkled throughout *How to Write Funny*. Make sure the funny part comes last, contrast is heightened to its maximum potential, needless words are omitted, it's simple, there's only one impossible thing, etc. If it passes muster, advance this joke to the next step. If it doesn't, try to edit it, but remember the First Laugh. If you have to change the wording so much that it becomes unrecognizable from its original form, you've likely destroyed the joke, which can easily happen at this stage. If you can't rework it simply without rewriting it entirely, it's best to reject it.

$$\left(\begin{array}{c} \text{I} + \\ \text{funny} \\ \text{filter} \end{array} \right) \times \text{subtext} - \begin{array}{c} \text{needless} \\ \text{words} \end{array} +$$

4. The joke makes you laugh after you forget it.

The best way to look at your ideas is to let them sit for a week or two and forget about them. This wait time provides a powerful perspective when looking at your own work. It mimics the perspective of the reader, which is the only perspective that matters. Readers are far more disinterested in your material than you might imagine. By putting yourself in their shoes, the harsh light of objective reality will show you which ideas have merit and which don't. If it genuinely makes you laugh after you've forgotten about it, that's a great sign. Advance to number five.

5. The joke has "legs."

A joke with "legs" can go somewhere. Sometimes you need to abandon your funniest concepts when you realize they can't go anywhere, or that they'll fall apart as soon as they're expanded into a longer piece of writing. Or sometimes the entirety of the joke is revealed in the concept, and there's nothing left to say in a longer piece. Other times the comedy world that's created by your concept, once you extrapolate it, just doesn't hold up.

Look for a title that introduces a comedy world, a world you can imagine more details about the more you think about it. A good concept begins to flourish when you ask yourself, "If this title is true, what else is true?" and the answers come easily. The comedy world your title opens up becomes so clear, other ideas that fit into it pop into your head quickly and easily. You begin to imagine all the funny things that will likely come out of this concept. This is a sign you've landed on the right concept.

This means the idea has legs, and you can run with it.

Be sure the title you select meets all of these criteria. If it only meets one or two, you probably have a dud.

AVOIDING BAD IDEAS

Most of the ideas you write—most of the ideas any of us write—will be bad, and knowing which ideas are bad, and avoiding them as source material for full comic pieces, is crucial to making this process work efficiently.

Go through this checklist on your final, selected ideas, and discard stories that meet *any* of the following criteria on this Title Rejection Gauntlet:

1. It's the wrong target.

Remember the tip in *How to Write Funny*, "Comfort the Afflicted, Afflict the Comfortable." Your joke must punch up. If it punches down, even if a few people laugh at it, it's probably the wrong target. And while your peers may laugh at it because certain punch-down jokes will work in an intimate setting between friends, they almost never work in a public forum.

2. It's been done before.

Google your joke. See if anyone has done anything too similar. If they have, scrap it. If anyone in your circle says it reminds them of other jokes they've heard, ask for details and then compare. If your idea seems too similar, scrap it. Originality is paramount to success in comedy writing.

FUNNIER-WRITING TIP #4: CREATE A COMEDY WORLD

When writing a comedy piece, be conscious of the fact that you're creating a new comedy world that's never been seen before. The world created by a comedy piece usually has one thing in it that's askew from the real world. If more than one element is askew, it risks confusing the reader (violating the "one impossible thing" tip from How to Write Funny*). Get in the habit of identifying and articulating the one impossible thing in your world as soon as you identify a good title for a piece. You'll need to understand and describe the comedy world you're creating when you start your first draft.*

---

3. You've already started writing it.

If you came to this book with a concept already in the hopper, and maybe even a few drafts or a few paragraphs written, please scrap it. At the very least, save it for later. This is all-too-common baggage beginning writers carry. They're mired in a draft that represents the one concept they have, the one they fell in love with, a concept that hasn't been tested or vetted as suggested here. Often, the piece isn't working, so it makes sense that they're stuck.

You might think it's a good use of your time to apply what you learn here to finish a previous piece of writing, the unfinished draft of which was been haunting you for weeks, months, or perhaps years. Quite the contrary—finishing that piece is a waste of your time. This book walks you through a process of selecting the best concepts and writing many, many pieces, all in a fraction of the time you may have already spent on that one piece.

Start fresh. It's a lot easier to launch a new boat from the dock than dredge up an old one from the ocean floor, repair it, and then try to set sail.

4. It's too long.

Shakespeare said, "Brevity is the soul of wit." Sometimes a joke can be too long to be a title for a piece. Or a concept can take too long to explain. A joke or concept of 5–10 words or less is ideal—this length appeals to almost anyone in your audience. If an idea is more than 10 or 15 words, you run the risk of people forgetting the beginning before they get to the end. And rest assured, very few people will read it twice to make sure they understood it. If they don't immediately get it, they'll move on to other writing that's easier to digest.

A MAN WITH A CARDBOARD BOX

Here's an example of the title-selection process:

The original joke, written by Robert Ward, was "Man Flattening Cardboard Boxes Wonders If This Is What True Power Really Feels Like." Robert selected the title from a list of 16 ideas. Other ideas on the list that were passed over were "World Population to Reach 10 Billion Idiots by 2080," "Someone With a Dog as Their Profile Photo Offers Their Condolences," among others.

The cardboard-box idea was selected because it passed through the Title Approval Gauntlet successfully:

1. It has Subtext: The feeling when you're flattening a cardboard box gives you a little power rush.

2. It uses several Funny Filters (Character, Reference, Irony, and Madcap) and it uses them properly: A simple character (the Everyman archetype), a relatable little observation from real life, excellent heightened contrast for good Irony, and a little bit of Madcap in the physical business of flattening a box, which would come out nicely if executed well.

3. The joke conforms with the best practices of a short joke: it's not a cliché, it's concise, it saves the funny part for last, it's simple, it's accessible,

it doesn't punch down, and it only has one impossible idea.

4. Robert thought the joke was funny.

5. The joke has legs. Seeing this man try to flatten a box and subtly act out the feeling of power we all feel when smashing a cardboard box has potential.

The joke also survived the Title Rejection Gauntlet:

1. The target of the joke is an average, suburban American man, a dad type who is absolutely a deserving target of ridicule.

2. After a Google search, Robert determined the idea was original.

3. He hadn't started writing it or been slaving at it for months. It was a fresh idea on a new list.

4. It's a little long, but not so long it's confusing. However, Robert and his feedback group determined it had too many needless words, so it was reduced to "Man Flattening Cardboard Box Tastes True Power."

Once a few of your concepts pass muster through both of these gauntlets, you're almost ready to select one to write. But before you do, there's one more important step that needs to be added to these Title Gauntlets. For that step, we'll explore the value of feedback from others to vet your concepts. This is one of the most critical yet overlooked steps in choosing the right concepts for comedy writing, and it deserves its own chapter.

CHAPTER 4 ACTION STEP

Compile a list of all the jokes, concepts, headlines, and one-liners you've come up with—these are potential titles for your comedy pieces. You should have dozens of them. Whittle them down to your best 10 or 20 using the process in the Title Gauntlets.

5

DON'T BE A LONE WOLF

Maybe you're blessed with an amazing, innate comic ability. Maybe you're a one-in-a-million talent whose every utterance and every scribble is comedy gold.

Not likely.

I don't mean to insult you. Decades in the business have shown me time and again that every great comedy writer or performer is someone who put in the work and dedication necessary to learn the craft. Innate "talent" had nothing to do with it. And in comedy, learning the craft doesn't mean doing it alone; it means involving others.

A great talent, therefore, is someone who writes hundreds of ideas and learns over time which ideas make people laugh and which ones don't. Most comedy writers learn this by testing jokes on people, getting feedback from peers, doing stand-up in front of real audiences, and suffering the occasional bombing. After a while (usually many years) they gain experience that gives them a strong sense of what works and what sucks.

These are the geniuses.

Writing, especially comedy writing, is often depicted in pop culture as a solitary affair, the intense thinker (a lone, talented genius) lost in thought, tapping feverishly on a trusty manual typewriter. The genius is inspired in a split second, then pulls the paper from the typewriter and presents the work to the boss, client, or peers, and the reaction is always the same: "Why, this is genius!"

That's not the way it works.

This unspoken but widely accepted myth hurts people who've subconsciously internalized it, leaving them wondering why they're suffering in front of a keyboard by themselves, staring at a blank screen, unable to produce anything—let alone anything "genius." Or worse, this myth stops people from even trying to write comedy because they believe if only they had the necessary "talent," amazing words would pour out of their minds in "flow state" as if produced by the lone geniuses of lore.

It's true that a writer mostly works alone. We first have to churn out raw material, then switch to our Editor brain, running our raw material through the qualifying gauntlets.

But that's only the first half of the process—the loneliest half. And the material generated during this process is far from genius. In fact, it's mostly garbage.

The other half of the process involves presenting your work to other people and get their feedback in order to see if any of your jokes work. Investing time writing a piece based on a concept no one else has seen is a waste of time. Without outside, objective confirmation, there's a 90-percent chance you've chosen a concept that's garbage.

We're still only in the concept selection stage. You've done your best to assess which jokes will make the best short pieces, but now you're bringing in the cavalry to help, because this selection process is too important to rely solely on your own judgement.

You may have a bias for your own title, even if you've set the idea aside long enough to forget it. You may even be one of the myriad of anxiety-ridden comedy writers or over-developed-Editor-brain types with a bias *against* your title. Either way, your subjective opinion of your own title ideas is of little value. It may be a "you had to be there" joke. Or it may just be something that tickles your funny bone but won't resonate with anyone else. The best way to eliminate any possibility of the contamination of your own subjectivity when judging titles is to get actionable opinions from other people. This is a complicated and fraught process.

When showing your jokes to others, you continue to use the Clown and Editor, but this time you re-assign the roles. Now you're the Clown and other people are temporarily the Editor. You do this by adding one more step to the Title Approval Gauntlet from the previous chapter:

6. The joke makes other people laugh.

Do your trusted confidants laugh out loud at your title without requiring any additional explanation from you? If so, advance to the next step.

Next, you need to add two more steps to the Title Rejection Gauntlet from the previous chapter:

5. The joke confuses people.

If you recite your title to other people (or they read it) and most of them give you a puzzled look, your title should be scrapped. Confusion is the enemy of comedy. If it takes you more than a sentence to explain the idea, at which point they laugh, then you may need to simply shorten the joke. If the joke makes them laugh a second or two after they hear it, then you have a "thinker" on your hands. That's good! But if the confusion lingers and people don't get your joke, it needs to be scrapped.

6. No one likes it but you.

It's important to have a strong internal barometer for what works for you and your unique comedic voice, but it must always be balanced against what appeals to potential audiences. A lot of beginning writers love their one idea, but they haven't tested it by reading it aloud to others, so it hasn't been properly vetted. And, more often than not, the concept is not strong. Before you write one word of a comedy piece, save your time and work smart by testing your title to make sure a lot of other people find it hilarious. Comedy is not art or uncritical self-expression. It's entertainment. Comedy only works if other people laugh. If they don't, you might have something else—maybe art—but it's not comedy.

On the balance of art and comedy, I don't mean to bash art. Well, maybe a little. I prefer comedy—it's funnier. But if all you want to create is art, feel free to sit at your computer and type away without ever showing your work to anyone. Maybe you'll get published in a literary quarterly.

Creating comedy requires you to come out of your shell. You need to show your jokes to other people. You need to listen to their feedback and unbridled criticism, then go back and reassess your work with the new understanding gained from their reaction.

A lot of us have a strange sense of humor. What makes us laugh when we're sitting at home alone in front of a computer might be far afield from anything that will connect with a real audience. Only when presenting your work to others do you stand a chance of knowing whether your writing achieves the most fundamental requirement of comedy: getting laughs.

THE FEEDBACK PROCESS

The feedback process is one of the biggest areas of misunderstanding in comedy. How exactly should you show your work to other people to get useful, constructive notes enabling you to improve your work quickly, efficiently, and properly? Some feedback can leave you spinning your wheels. Other feedback, however, can zero in on your weaknesses and excise them like a cancer, putting you on a fast track to professional-caliber comedy writing.

Showing your work to others when first starting out can be difficult. In fact, it can be terrifying. If you've never done it before and you're afraid of it, the best way to conquer this fear is to face it. Realize no harm will come to you by showing your work. Tell yourself it's no big deal. If you think it will hurt too much if people have a negative reaction, realize they'll still like you. Get used to the feeling. Make the plunge. That's really the only way to do it. You won't get far hiding your work.

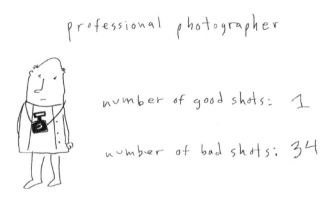

If you're daunted by this step, here's an idea to take some of the pressure off, and possibly give you a different mindset. One of my students, Bill, came up with a fitting analogy for how to think about this part of the comedy writing process. Photographers routinely take dozens and dozens of photos in order to find a good one. Everyone seems to understand this process when it relates to photography. The photographer's peers understand it, and they happily offer feedback, pointing out which photo among the pile are keepers. Despite the fact that only a tiny percentage of the photos are deemed acceptable, at no point does anyone question the photographer's skill at taking good photos. And the photographer isn't scared to show the work. Getting feedback in this context isn't perceived as a personal attack like it can be with comedy writing. On the contrary, most people, photographers and otherwise, accept that picking "selects" is just part of the process.

Be the photographer. Welcome help from your peers. No matter how critical they are of the 90 percent that you'll toss out, they're doing you a favor, helping you find your best 10 percent that you'll present to the world.

Regardless of any fear you might have, getting feedback that's useful can be extremely difficult. Almost anyone can get their roommate or mom to read their list of ideas, but your roommate or mom will likely muster a polite laugh and tell you that your work is pretty good. Conversely, they may hate everything you write, which is a different problem altogether. Either way, this is not useful feedback.

You need to show your work to someone who will critique it constructively, someone who will say, "These parts are working and made me laugh, these other parts, or the idea behind it, weren't very funny, but here are some ideas for how you could improve it." Only a professional humor writer or editor, or someone who is uncommonly adept at offering criticism to other writers, will be capable of giving you this kind of feedback.

If you don't have access to a group of such people, here are some ideas for cobbling one together:

FINDING YOUR TEAM

Finding people to give you quality feedback has never been easier. You can join a local or online writers group, take a comedy writing class, take an improv class, or seek out friends who also write. Do any or all of these things and you're sure to meet people who understand your sensibility and can offer honest, constructive notes.

Plenty of online writers groups and writer-feedback forums welcome your submissions. As of this writing, some of the most prominent are critiquecircle.com, absolutewrite.com, mibba.com, nanowrimo.com (for longer-form work), thenextbigwriter.com, and reddit.com/write. Of course online feedback has its own problems. Yes, they're strangers, so now their feedback will be more objective, but by the same token, you don't know them, and you can't assess their opinions against their sensibilities or prejudices like you can with friends, family, and peers.

These are all legitimate places to hunt for people who can provide quality feedback. You'll have to try them out and see if they can give you the honest and constructive notes you need.

THE FOUR LEVELS OF FEEDBACK

What follows are four different levels of feedback. Assess your peers and determine what level of feedback they offer. It's best to find a mix of more objective, potentially heartless (and ultimately more useful) feedback online with more polite (yet possibly more engaged) feedback in person. Only then will you build a useful "writers room" or group of peers, virtual or in-person, who can help make your writing funnier.

1. Level One Feedback: Reactions to jokes from friends and family, whether you show them written jokes or put together a makeshift performance to read jokes aloud. This kind of feedback is primarily intended to avoid hurting your feelings. It rarely helps you improve. Sometimes, depending on the relationship you have with the person giving the feedback, it can be the opposite; it can be incredibly blunt and painfully negative, but still equally unhelpful. Your mom is most often trying to support you or undermine you. Your friend or sibling, who's always there to cut you down with a little good-natured ribbing, may sit stone-faced, either unimpressed at your attempts or jealous of your courage to write. In both cases, the feedback is hopelessly biased. Members of this group know you too well. They can't be expected to extract their intimate knowledge of you from their perception of your work, but they must in order to provide useful feedback. A potential reader finding your work online doesn't

know you, so they'll judge your work on its merits alone. This is something your friends and family simply aren't able to do.

And these are just the problems with the audience. Many problems come from you, especially if you're reading your jokes out loud. How confident is your bearing when you're reading your jokes? How tense are you? Are you speaking like a mouse or a practiced public speaker? An audience's reaction to a performer—even in an informal setting—has very little to do with the material being presented; it has almost everything to do with the self-assuredness of the person presenting it. The only way to remove this factor from a Level One Feedback scenario is to present your jokes in writing. But even this approach exposes the problems of personal bias.

2. Level Two Feedback: Critical reaction to your work from comedy peers. If you've met other people with similar humor sensibilities or who also write comedy, and they've agreed to give honest feedback on your work, this is an opportunity to get more constructive feedback than Level One.

However, many of the same problems you encounter with Level One feedback plague Level Two as well: these people may have a bias for or against you, skewing their view of your work; they may treat you with kid gloves or be unnecessarily harsh. But with Level Two feedback, you at least have a little more control over the situation than with Level One. Level Two people at least understand your work from a production standpoint, and you might be able to engage them in thoughtful conversations about what's working and what isn't.

And because you know these people personally, you can segment their feedback based on what you know about them, giving you a little more power to contextualize it.

The biggest flaw of this group is that they'll pay far greater attention to your work than a real audience will. Real audiences don't pay close attention. They might see your work in a few fleeting seconds, but they aren't going to dwell on it. Peers who read your work carefully and give you detailed feedback are a treasure, but realize that this makes their reaction an extremely poor approximation of the anonymous reader's experience.

FUNNIER HUMOR WRITING TIP #5: READERS AREN'T PAYING ATTENTION

When it comes to getting critical feedback on your work, one thing both you and your feedback group are likely to forget is that real readers will never pay as close attention to your work as you or your feedback group will. Real readers will, in fact, barely notice that it exists. If you somehow mange to catch their attention and entice them to read further, they'll pay closer attention to your written piece, at least at first, and they may keep reading if your prose is engaging enough. But when it comes to the title, potential readers have, at best, a fleeting interaction with you. This context is the opposite of how anyone in your feedback group is likely to interact with your joke. They'll often read it carefully, several times, and then ponder its effectiveness. Such care and attention, though heartwarming, is counterproductive. They're not approximating the reader's experience, and therefore not providing representative feedback. A flippant, off-the-cuff response to your joke from someone in your feedback group is often far more valuable than a thoughtful and in-depth one.

Level Three Feedback: Showing your work in a writers forum online. With this level of feedback, you're removing yourself and your biased relationship with the audience from the equation and getting an honest, real reaction. It's closer to what you'd expect from a real audience. This is a different beast altogether from Levels One and Two. Now you're being judged by readers who don't know you. Equally important, you don't know them either. Their specific sense of humor is a mystery, so catering to them or playing to their tastes isn't an option. You're forced to make your material more accessible in order to get any kind of positive reaction.

Post your jokes on a writers forum or one of the feedback sites I mentioned above. If you have a budget, submit jokes to a testing app like pickfu.com.

Finding a group of people to review your work who don't know you personally is extremely valuable.

Granted, people in this group may still give your work undue attention, which puts them on the same plane as Level Two feedback folks when it comes to approximating a real reader's experience. But at least they're strangers who aren't invested in your success. That's important.

One flaw of this group worth noting is that many writer forums have rules of civility, encouraging people to pull their punches in the same way a group of friends or in-person peers might, which is unfortunate. Sometimes what a comedy writer needs to hear is, "That idea is awful!" And that kind of refreshing honesty can get users flagged on online forums.

I administer a private Facebook group [https://www.facebook.com/groups/howtowritefunny/] for experienced joke writers to provide feedback on other members' jokes. Professional comedy writers and I chime in frequently. This is an excellent place to test out jokes, so I encourage you to join. If you're reading this book, you'll ace the secret question to get access.

4. Level Four Feedback: Presenting your work to actual audiences. A skeptical audience of real people are the best qualified to objectively assess your writing. The harsh truth is that people don't want to read your writing. They don't care about it. Only you and your friends care about it. Real audiences are tough, and that's the audience you need to wow if you're going to succeed.

Post potential titles on Twitter. If people don't like your jokes, they won't hit the "like" button or retweet them, which tells you a lot. If you have almost no followers and almost none of your tweets get a reaction, you'll know when you've written a funny joke because one or two people will like it.

Read your jokes at an open mic. Stand-up audiences are the toughest audiences of all, and typically the most honest.

I realize the idea of getting on stage to read jokes is a terrifying prospect to a lot of people, even those who strive to get better at writing comedy. So

I understand why some would never consider this option. But if you want to improve quickly, consider it. The crucible experienced from facing your fear of performing comedy will unlock an important door in your life, both professionally and personally. Getting on stage can be transformative. It can boost your confidence, make you more comfortable in your own skin, and give you something to feel good about for the rest of your life. Besides that, it's some the best feedback you can get.

The serious comedy professional trusts the Level Four feedback group above all, but the best way to use these different levels of feedback is to create tiers and then compare results. First, assess your concepts on your own. Then show them to your roommate or mom. Then to your peer group at Levels Two and Three. Then execute them according to the process outlined in this book. Once you have a short piece, sketch, or stand-up bit, bring it to a Level Four audience. You'll get useful feedback at every level to improve your jokes. The more you go through every part of this process, the more you'll learn, and the better you'll get.

Once you have a writers group or a collection of peers, you need to train them to be brutally honest. This may take some time and, ultimately, may not work. Cultivating a great group is possible, though, and *How to Write Funniest*, the third book in this series, will focus entirely on building a comedy team to maximize the brain power of a group to produce stellar comedy. But for now, begin building your team according to the tips in this chapter.

You can learn and grow as a comedy writer without going through this feedback process. But you'll learn less and it will take a lot longer. If you're working on something important, like a piece you plan to submit to a publication or agent, or if you're planning to go into production on a project based on one of your concepts, that's when it's absolutely critical to go through this entire feedback process and make sure you're putting your hard work into only your most hilarious concepts. Don't just trust your instincts. This is the most common mistake amateur comedy writers make. They come up with one idea, fall in love with it, fail to vet it with any peer feedback, and then invest a lot of time, money, and effort executing a video, screenplay, or web series. The result? A project that's not nearly as good as it could've been if a tiny fraction of the time (and none of the money) had been invested earlier in the process. Getting thorough feedback on ideas from competent peers cannot be overlooked.

It's a good idea to get a good mix of people in your feedback group, some young, some old, some experienced, some not, etc. You want to approximate the potential audience, and by getting feedback that's sure to be varied, you'll know when you've hit on a great idea if all the people in your feedback group like it.

WHEN YOU HATE YOUR OWN JOKES

One pitfall in the feedback process worth noting is that sometimes your funniest ideas are ones you're not particularly fond of. Maybe you think they're too easy or too crass. This happens a lot. Even if you don't like them, if they pass all the criteria of the Title Gauntlets, include those ideas on your Shortlist. Be generous to yourself. If you really hate it, if it's just not in your voice or you don't feel comfortable writing it, that's your prerogative and you should scrap it. But if people love it and you can live with it or learn to like it, it's worth writing, if only for the experience. Being attuned to how people respond to your material and noticing how that's different from how you respond to it, is a great way to discover your unique voice as a writer.

And play it forward. When asked, provide feedback to others pursuing comedy. Even if they don't ask, you should offer. All it takes is a few minutes of your time to review their work, and you can make a huge impact on their success. There's plenty of room in the comedy business for everyone to be funny, and we should all be happy for each other's success. But if you don't feel that way and only care about your own success, consider this: the person you help today may be in a position to offer you a job tomorrow. It always pays to be nice.

If we all work together to help each other in the comedy business, the comedy produced, including yours, will only get funnier. This is an investment in future laughs we can all feel good about.

Ostensibly, this book is about how to write a short-form comedy piece. It's no accident that many of these first chapters have been focused on how to choose the right concept. Choosing the right concept for your piece is by far the most important step in the process of writing comedy. You have to know the core joke of your piece, and your reader has to know the core joke of your piece, and you have to be as sure as you can be that it's funny.

A good concept—even poorly written—will often succeed with audiences. But a bad concept—even if written beautifully and perfectly—will often fail.

Choosing the right concept is also the most efficient action you can take to make sure you succeed. A good concept is another fulcrum you can use to get leverage, working smarter instead of harder. Before you spend hours slaving over a piece of writing, make sure the concept you're executing is the most hilarious one you can come up with, one that's unquestionably worthy of your time and effort. This is how you increase your ratio of successful to unsuccessful work.

CHAPTER 5 ACTION STEPS

1. Enlist people to be in your feedback group.

2. Run all your title ideas by members of your feedback group.

3. Make a Shortlist of all the ideas that were liked by members of your feedback group and that you're also excited about writing. This is the list of short comedy pieces you're ready to start drafting.

6

KEEP YOUR PROMISE

Now that you have your concept, which comes in the form of a title, and you're confident that it's worthy of being expanded based on feedback, it's time to write it.

In 1889, Russian playwright Anton Chekhov gave some storytelling advice to another writer. He said, "If in the first act you have hung a pistol on the wall, then in the following one it should be fired. Otherwise don't put it there."

Scriptwriters and playwrights have been dogged by this advice for decades. "Chekov's Gun" is one of the most frequently cited rules of storytelling. Writers take it to mean that everything in a story should be there for a reason. If you show the audience something, understand that they'll expect it to be integral to your story. They trust you know what you're doing, not wasting their time setting up unimportant details that aren't going to pay off in some satisfying way later on.

Steven Spielberg updated Chekov's Gun in the 1980s. The rule wasn't big enough for Spielberg. He knew the rule, of course, and abided by it faithfully, but he took it one step further. In the age of billion-dollar blockbusters, audiences had begun to expect more. The rule I'm dubbing "Spielberg's Life Raft" was unofficially adopted in 1987 in *Indiana Jones and the Temple of Doom*. Indy and his friends had to jump out of an airplane before it crashed into the side of a mountain, but there were no parachutes. They did, however, find an inflatable life raft onboard. The raft inflated as they jumped, then landed on a snow-covered mountainside, bounced to a stop, and miraculously coasted them to safety. But because Spielberg had introduced a life raft, he was now obliged to follow Chekhov's Gun rule and show the life raft in a whitewater rafting sequence. But, it wouldn't be just any whitewater rafting sequence. It would have to be the most spectacular white-water rafting scene ever filmed. The audience was made to believe Indy and his friends had coasted to safety, but at the last second their life raft fell off an impossibly high cliff into a raging river. This was the new, unspoken rule. The bar had been raised. Spielberg knew it, and so did the audience.

If audiences don't get what they expect from their entertainment, you, the entertainer, have let them down, and your work will be considered a failure. If audiences get what they expect, they're pleased. But Chekhov's Gun is just the minimum requirement. If you really want to delight audiences, give them Spielberg's Life Raft. Over-deliver by giving them what they expect, but in the best possible way. This is especially true in comedy, where surprise is the commodity.

While we're primarily dealing with comedy structure and not dramatic story structure in this book, Chekhov's Gun and Spielberg's Life Raft are important rules to remember. Following Chekhov's is required; following Spielberg's is the secret to making audiences fall in love with your writing.

In the subconscious recesses of your reader's mind, your title has set up your premise and introduced the core joke that you'll be elaborating on in your written piece. When readers laugh at your title, you've made a connection with them. This connection is a commitment. You've teased them with a taste of the comedy world that awaits them if they decide to read your piece.

Funnier-Writing Tip #6: Deliver the Expected Unexpectedly

Readers will expect a certain type of joke, a certain tone, and a certain style of humor from your title. You must deliver on these expectations, but you can't deliver in an expected way. After all, the essential ingredient in all humor is surprise. How do you find the balance between giving the audience what they expect while also surprising them? If you don't surprise them enough, they'll be bored. If you surprise them too much, they'll be confused. The trick is to ask yourself what they expect from your title. Ask your feedback group for answers too. Make a list of the major expectations you uncover, written out not as jokes, but simply as descriptions of the expectations. Next, come up with original jokes that fulfill those expectations. You'll add those jokes to the pile of potential jokes to include in your piece.

This commitment is the prose equivalent of a movie poster or book cover. Remember that the vast majority of your audience is not paying close attention. They're interested in things that momentarily and absent-mindedly attract them. In the case of movie posters and book covers, this happens in a split second, on a subliminal level. Even before reading any of the words, they've decided whether they're interested. Marketing experts and graphic designers know this, and expend great effort communicating information about the movie or book using the right colors, fonts, and overall layout. Likewise, the title of a comedy piece communicates all the nuances the reader can expect. What are the Funny Filters? How dark is it? How smart does it seem? Your potential reader is unconsciously answering these questions, and then comparing the answers against their sense of humor. If it's a match, they might read your story. And if they do, they expect to get what was promised.

If a move poster has a black background and some kind of glowing, green shape or futuristic font on it, you know it's a science fiction movie.

If the poster has a white background and a picture of someone with bug eyes on it, you know it's a comedy. A movie poster's job is, first and foremost, to communicate the movie's genre. Genres are important because they tell people, in the first milliseconds—before they've even registered a single word of the poster—what kind of movie they can expect. And they'll expect plenty of genre tropes in those movies. If the movies are good, those tropes will appear in unexpected ways, ways the audience has never seen before.

> FUNNIER-WRITING TIP #7: YOUR TITLE IS A PROMISE
> *The tile of your piece introduces your comedy world to readers. If they like it and laugh at it, they'll want more where that came from. They'll want to read your story and get more jokes like the title, and they'll want to see it expanded and keep getting bigger, better, and funnier. Why? Because you've successfully seduced them into reading your piece. They want to be satisfied. Now the hard work begins: You must live up to that promise. You have to tell the story they unconsciously expect from your headline. If you go in a different direction, or don't make good on your promise, they'll be disappointed and will bail on your piece. But if you fulfill your promise and continue to delight them with the same vein of humor your title suggested—if you can deliver Spielberg's Life Raft—they'll keep reading.*

Your title communicates the genre of your joke. For example, if your story is about sex, or has an F-bomb in it, then it's a Shock-based story. So, your story has to be shocking. If you write a story that's not shocking, readers will abandon you after a few lines. If you deliver the most hilariously shocking piece ever, they'll remember you.

These rules are easy to understand but extremely difficult to follow. Striking the proper balance between what's expected by the audience and what's out of bounds for them is a skill that comes with practice. The fundamental rule of Chekhov's Gun is violated all the time in short prose.

A writer will do the good work of vetting a concept—they'll chose a wonderful and hilarious title—but then the written piece fails to deliver on the most basic expectations of their promise. It's unrelated, or drifts off track, has the wrong kinds of jokes, or otherwise doesn't meet the audience's demands.

A title that isn't funny is where 99 percent of humor writers fail. And of the one percent who manage to come up with a hilarious title, about 99 percent of them will fail by writing a bad story to follow it up.

Many of the rungs on the ladder of a successful humor piece are shaky and perilous. You must proceed with caution. Here are three questions to ask yourself before taking the next step. Once you answer, you'll have trusty rails to cling to as you work your way up the ladder, making sure you're in the top 1 percent of the 1 percent who make it all the way up and produce a short comedy piece that actually makes people laugh:

1. What's your medium?

One of the biggest mistakes I see with a lot of beginning writers is that they chose the wrong medium for their idea. Sometimes their idea is potentially funny, but by executing it in the wrong medium, the joke isn't given its best chance to shine. Give your concept the attention it deserves before you start writing by asking the simple question: "What is the best medium for my message?" Will this funny concept you've come up with be best executed as a story? A stand-up bit? A video sketch? Which medium do you have access to? You want to utilize whatever resources available to put your work in the best possible light and offer it up for the widest distribution, and the right medium plays a central role in that effort. Run it through in your mind in each of the seven media (prose, stage, TV/web video, movies, audio/podcast, visual, and street art) and see how you like it in each. Here are some example mediums and guidelines for selecting them:

Prose: Just about any idea can be executed in the form of a short prose piece, but some are more naturally suited to this medium. You should write your idea as a prose piece if it's subtle, literary, not very visual, or if it's likely to include a lot of Wordplay that won't translate well in a visual or auditory medium. If you have a parody of another form of writing such as a certain author's voice, a teen magazine, a suicide note, or a press release—anything that's a prose medium to begin with—readers will expect your piece to use prose.

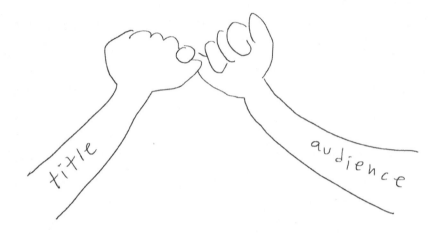

Video: If your piece is dialog heavy, if the main thrust of it is a conversation, or the dynamics of people talking, or if it's dependent on any silly physical action (Madcap) or location, a video sketch is probably going to be the best fit. If you're parodying an existing TV/video format, then audiences will expect you to present it as a sketch. Write it as a script or in short-story format (with dialog in quotes), or produce it as an online video. If you can't afford to shoot a live video, consider animating it, which is much less expensive. Also, crude, inexpensive animation is funny.

Visual: If simple visuals are necessary to get your joke, or if images will make it markedly funnier, consider creating it as a cartoon or meme. A multi-panel cartoon uses the same structure as a written prose piece. Each panel is a different beat (called a "joke beat") in the escalation of your core joke. Don't worry that you can't draw. Some of the best, most celebrated cartoonists in recent years have confessed their lack of skills in that area. All that matters in cartooning is writing. But if the drawing is important to you, find an illustrator who draws in a style you like.

Stage: Almost any joke can be told in a stand-up bit. Like prose, the stage is an extremely flexible medium. If it's a rant, monologue, or funny opinion, stand-up is perfect. If it's based on strong observational Subtext, all the better.

Audio: if you've written a sketch but find it too expensive to produce, consider creating an audio sketch. Maybe it's a scene in a jungle, which will be impossible to shoot since you don't live near a jungle. Sound Effects of jungles are a lot cheaper than getting yourself and a crew to a jungle location.

You be the judge of how your idea works best. Keep an open mind. Don't feel as though you have to limit yourself to one medium. The most important thing is that you keep an open mind. The medium you chose shouldn't be arbitrary. It should be the medium in which your funny idea will be the funniest.

2. What's your format?

Once you've decided on the medium for your piece, determine the best format. Let's say you've settled on prose. Within that medium, as in the others, there are countless formats to chose from. Here are some examples:

A first-person essay: If your idea consists largely of an opinion or quotes from one character, a first-person essay is probably the best format. However, if it's your opinion laid bare with no Subtext, consider expressing the opinion through a Funny Filter. For example, use Irony by expressing the comic opposite of your opinion, or use Character by expressing the opinion through the voice of a fictional character. (See *The Colbert Report*.)

A short story: If your idea has characters who learn something or whose actions affect the actions of other characters, it's probably best to execute using dramatic structure in the form of a short story. If your concept is bigger than a short story, it could be a novel. But I recommend you start with a short story if you're a beginner. I'll go into Dramatic Structure in detail in chapter 16.

A listicle: Articles that come in the form of lists are a popular format for short humor. If your idea is simply a running list of funny things, this format is ideal. Each item on your list can be made funnier when accompanied by an image and a little paragraph of prose.

A parody of a particular piece of writing: Maybe you want to write a parody of a bestselling book, but applied to a silly subject, like "E L James Writes Yelp Reviews."

Some of the most popular formats in satire at the moment are advertising, newswriting, women's magazine writing, and clickbait articles. But of course you can parody any style or format imaginable. Which is best for your idea? If, for example, your idea is a mechanic who lies about car repairs, you might want to write that in the form of a parody of a bill from an auto-repair shop.

3. What's your take?

At this point in the process of writing a short humor piece, you need to ask yourself, "What's my take on this piece?" The "take" is your approach, your angle, the track you escalate on. I'll get into more detail on what a track is in the next chapter, and escalation will be explained in chapter 10. For now, think of the take as the direction you're taking the humor. Another way to think about the take is applying the language of improv: What's the game of your scene? What is the one unusual thing audiences will want to see being spooled out and escalated, and how will it be spooled out? That's your take.

Getting the right take for a piece is difficult. Sometimes writing an entire first draft and showing it to your feedback group is necessary to learn your piece had the wrong take. When that happens, you need to do a complete rewrite. The take is that important.

To determine the take of a piece, write down all the ideas that spring from your funny title based on the expectations you believe your reader has. When your feedback group reviews your concept, write down any joke suggestions they have that spring from it. These notes provide clues to the most promising take for your piece. Most of the time, the funniest ideas that emerge from this brainstorming indicate what your take should be. You're looking for the richest vein of jokes that get not only to the heart of your reader's expectations, but also to the heart of your Subtext.

Always come back to your title when determining the take, and make sure you're staying on course. The right take is more important than a random funny idea that's "off-take." A lot of the suggestions coming from you and others will be "off-take"; they won't live up to your audience's expectations based on the title that lured them in. When the right take is achieved, when a piece is "on take," it delivers exactly the kind of humor the audience wants and expects.

We'll delve more into how to find the right take in the next chapter.

FUNNIER-WRITING TIP #8: GET THE RIGHT TAKE

A story can be written in a number of different ways. How is the humor in your joke escalated? What's the angle? What's the best direction to take your idea? Your answers to these questions will help you define the take. The right take is the most ideal combination of direction, angle, and approach, and it's one of the most difficult parts of the comedy writing process. It often requires peer review and more than one draft. But your piece won't work until you've found the right take. Often, a clue to the right take can be found by carefully looking at the title and remembering the First Laugh. What does the title imply? What is it promising? What exactly did people find funny about it? What will they expect from the piece? Answering these questions will put you on track to find the right take.

Returning to the example of Robert's cardboard-box piece, let's see how he answered the questions in this chapter.

The medium chosen for the piece was mixed: video and prose. Video would allow the Madcap of the moment to play out. Prose would be best for describing the relatable moment and giving it the heightened contrast needed for maximum laughs. With the right means, he might have made a video sketch in which a world leader demonstrates his power by flattening a cardboard box at a press conference. But of course, that's a bigger production. A simple vérité video and a short prose piece was within his means and suited the idea well.

The format Robert chose was a parody of a news story, which would give the event gravitas. Featured online, it could use smartphone footage, as many online magazines do, of the man breaking down the cardboard box by the trash can behind his house. This would give it verisimilitude, looking exactly like a story in an online news publication.

For clues to the right take, Robert looked at his title. It uses the phrase "True Power." That idea must be taken seriously and followed through on. The take would be showing the man's real power, and the editorial voice and other characters in the story would genuinely accept that he's powerful simply based on his act of flattening a cardboard box. They should be impressed by him. This would allow Robert to heighten all four of the Funny Filters at work in his idea.

You'll see more examples of takes working and not working in subsequent chapters. For now, be sure your medium, format, and take align with your title. That's how you deliver on your promise to the reader.

CHAPTER 6 ACTION STEP

Figure out the medium, format, and take for your piece. What's the best way to hang jokes on it? What do people expect from it?

CREATE JOKE BEATS

Prose is the only medium that demands your audience's rapt attention. So, you're asking no small thing of them when you write a piece of comedy prose. You're asking them to shut out the cacophony of enticing, wonderful, exciting, thrilling, sexy, gut-wrenching, persuasive, heart-warming, and attention-grabbing noise that surrounds them every second and focus instead on your writing. You're asking them to give you—for free—one of the most valuable resources in our economy: their attention.

The focus of book one in this series, *How to Write Funny*, was the crafting of short one-liners that make people laugh. These are the "magnetic headlines" that are so valuable online and elsewhere for getting eyeballs. They're the hook that first grabs people's attention. You learned how to increase the size and strength of your hooks by using Subtext, the Funny Filters, co-opting other media, and turning your jokes into mixed media in order to increase the chance they'll get seen. You learned how to use design and layout to draw the reader in. You learned the power of visuals, video, and street art. *How to Write Funny* encouraged you to think creatively, use any trick you can imagine, and break any rule to somehow get people to notice your work.

But these techniques, as powerful as they are, only hook people initially. They get people to read your short headline or an introductory snippet of your writing. But now, with your comedy piece, an even more difficult task lies ahead—to keep them reading, line after line, paragraph after paragraph.

You got their attention, now how do you keep it?

After the title catches them, one way to burrow your hook deeper is using the powerful emotional draw of dramatic structure. People love getting pulled into a good story. But another literary structure, one based not on drama but on comedy, can be just as powerful. With comedic structure, it's not emotional hooks that hold the audience's attention; it's jokes. Each new joke in the writing (each "joke beat") pulls your audience closer.

People don't put much effort or intellectual thought behind what they decide to read. They aren't paying close attention, at least not at first. Like a plane flying cross-country, your potential reader is on autopilot most of the time. When people shop for something to read, they're less like a human being and more like a kitten, just chasing movement. They're not thinking logically or critically about their choices. They're merely letting their lower brain make decisions based on what's attractive to them in the moment.

If they laughed at your title, they've bitten the hook, and you've made a catch. Joke beats allow you to reel them in. However, readers don't want your title joke repeated over and over. They'd lose interest in that immediately. They want to see your joke escalate and deepen.

That's why joke beats must be a continuation of the initial joke that attracted your audience in the first place—this is the line attached to your hook. If you start telling jokes that are off-take, you're pulling a random fishing line out of the water that's not attached to your hook, and your reader easily swims away.

Throughout a comedy piece, every few seconds, a new joke beat should appear. Each one should feel bigger and crazier than the beat before. Joke beats should come at least every two or three sentences in a written piece. They can also come more frequently, but any more than one per line might make the piece too dense, and this kind of joke-beat volume takes a lot of experience to pull off successfully. (See *30 Rock*.) You need to pace your story just right (roughly one joke beat per sentence) so the reader has time to laugh, enjoy the anticipation of the next joke beat, and then when it comes, laugh again. That's why the sober exposition and connective tissue between your joke beats is critical to the humor. Your writing must play it straight (but still exist firmly within your comedy world), and never wink or smirk at the audience. Act as if you have no awareness the piece is the least bit funny.

Most beginning writers don't have enough joke beats in their work. These pieces come off as misfires. Others try desperately to inject as many joke beats in their pieces as they can, or use a jokey tone, forgetting that it's the straight voice that creates the contrast for the jokes to work. These pieces come off as desperate. The best comedically structured stories have just the right balance between straight and funny.

What I'm describing here—hooking a reader with a piece and getting them to read through to the end—is difficult to accomplish. If an uninitiated reader finishes your piece, congratulations! You're in the top tier of comedy professionals. Even at *The Onion*, the most popular humor publication in the world, only about 15 percent of readers make it to the end of articles. (I know this from the heat maps our web analytics team showed us, revealing where readers clicked, and whether they scrolled down on pages.)

The quality of your joke beats is the secret to getting people to read to the end, and it's where most comedy stories—even those written by professionals—fall short.

By nailing joke beats, consistently making each one build and escalate your piece to the increasing delight of your audience, you've attained a level of skill that gets you hired on TV comedy shows. You even have a chance to achieve the kind of notoriety Simon Rich or *The Onion* did. The skill is that rare.

The reason most writers fall short is they don't brainstorm enough joke-beat ideas, so they don't create the quantity necessary to achieve the quality readers demand.

Once you've vetted your title and you know your take, you must go back to the process you went through writing jokes, making lists of dozens and dozens of them. Only now, your jokes must relate precisely to your title concept and serve the take of your piece. Make sure the jokes use the right Funny Filters determined by your structure, take, and expectations of the title. Yes, jokes must be new and different, but they can only be new and different within these parameters. In a way, it may feel like you're telling the same joke over and over. And, in a way, you will be, but each joke will be bigger, broader, have more at stake, or be said in a different, more elevated way, perhaps employing additional Funny Filters.

Funnier-Writing Tip #9: If This Is True, What Else Is True?

Here's a trick improvisers use to build a funny scene. It's a great way to come up with joke beats for your story, populate the comedy world your funny title creates, and make sure your jokes are on the same track as your title. Ask yourself "If this funny thing in my title is true, what else is true?" Then answer it using as many funny ideas as you can. This gives you a pool of potential joke beats from which to select the best.

RIFFING

After you figure out a structure for your concept, one of the best ways to create joke beats for it is through riffing. Riffing can also help you determine the medium, format, take and structure, but jokes beats is where riffing really shines.

Riffing is an off-the-top-of-your-head process no different from brainstorming jokes, but this time you're riffing on a theme—the topic of your title. You're in Clown mode while riffing, and it helps create quantity, which leads to quality. Riffing is a stream-of-consciousness exercise that should take you no more than 10–15 minutes to get the joke beats necessary for your piece. You can riff by yourself or with your feedback group. You can riff together in one place or do it virtually, where members of your feedback group send their riffs written out.

I prefer riffing virtually with my feedback groups. It results in well-thought-out, written joke-beat suggestions that are usually a higher quality than those spoken aloud in a group setting. It's easier to keep people on-take when they're riffing virtually, because they're not influenced by the comments of others. Also, I get a wider variety of ideas because there's no "group think." On the other hand, riffing in person has its benefits: one person's idea can spur another person's idea. If members of your feedback group have improv training, they can be especially productive in a group riffing session. You'll have to decide for yourself which method works best for you.

Each joke beat must be based on the joke in your title, which sets up and explains the funny situation of your piece, the one strange thing that's off in the comedy world you've created. Here are 10 questions to get the riffing going. Start with the funny situation in your title, then ask yourself or your group the following:

- How are other characters in this world reacting to this funny situation?
- What other groups in society could react to this funny situation?
- What are different ways the funny situation is manifesting?
- What are some other circumstances or contexts in which this funny situation might play out?
- What will happen with the funny situ-

ation if other characters, who might be diametrically opposed to it, come into contact with it?

- Could a famous person be associated with the funny situation, or could it get some notoriety in some way?
- What are some other times in the past this funny situation has happened?
- How did this funny situation start?
- How will this funny situation get worse, or better?
- How will this funny situation end, or will it be permanent?

To create additional joke beats, you can also run your title through the 11 Funny Filters, especially any Funny Filters used in the title, and use the Divining method described in *How to Write Funny* to come up with additional joke beats.

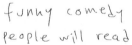

funny comedy people will read

unfunny comedy no one will read

A word of caution: it's easy to come up with jokes during the riffing process that are off-take, especially if you're getting help from your feedback group in person. People can easily start riffing off other people's wrong-take jokes, taking the conversation down the wrong road. But that's okay. You need to be in Clown mode when riffing. Later, you'll weed out the jokes that don't work. In a group, do your best to steer the feedback to stay on-take without pushing your team too far into Editor brain.

WHAT RIFFING LOOKS LIKE

Returning to the example of Robert's cardboard-box story, a lot of joke beats were brainstormed. Here are some of the joke beats he selected for the piece:

• He grunts in a powerful, beastly way when crushing the box.

• He snorts arrogantly and says something like "Who wants some?" to the box.

• He pancakes the boxes and feels emboldened.

• He has no power in any other part of his life.

Note how many of the brainstormed joke beats employ the same Funny Filters as the title (Madcap and Reference). Also note how they don't deviate from the central subject of the joke. Several more joke beats were brainstormed for the piece, but it only needs a handful. Below are some jokes that didn't make the cut, followed by an explanation:

REJECTED JOKE BEAT: He finds other things to make him feel powerful, like lifting his garage door.

WHY IT DOESN'T WORK: The title joke is about how it feels to break down a cardboard box, not lifting a garage door.

REJECTED JOKE BEAT: He turns into a super-villain.

WHY IT DOESN'T WORK: This veers too far from the Reference humor promised by the headline and becomes a different, more cartoonish world.

REJECTED JOKE BEAT: An Analogy with drugs, where nothing gives him the high of that first box

WHY IT DOESN'T WORK: An Analogy with drugs isn't implied in the headline, and is too far afield from the core joke.

This type of hyper-focus on the core joke of your title ensures you're selecting the best of the best from a list of joke beats. The more focused you can be on the core humor of your title and why it's working, the better.

CHAPTER 7 ACTION STEPS

1. Brainstorm dozens of joke beats for your piece. Base them on your title concept.

2. Ask members of your feedback group to review your joke-beat ideas.

3. Ask your feedback group to riff on your idea. If they do this for you in person, record them to capture every joke. (Taking notes is too slow and you'll miss too many.)

4. Select only the funniest jokes from your list and your feedback group's brainstorming session. These are the joke beats you'll use in your first draft.

8

IT'S THE JOKE, STUPID

People who write comedy tend to be smart. Most of the writers I hired and trained at *The Onion* were intimidatingly smart, with genius-level IQs.

A smart person can make incredible Wordplay jokes. They can find interesting connections between disparate ideas to make amazing Analogy jokes that everyone else wishes they'd thought of. They can see through bullshit and point out hypocrisy and therefore create Character and Irony. They also think a lot, so they're never at a loss for great Subtext.

Obviously being extremely intelligent is a plus in almost any endeavor in life. But in one key area of comedy, intelligence can be a liability.

In order for comedy to succeed, it needs to connect with an audience. Sometimes, when a writer of a comedy piece is super smart, the writing is too highbrow, and no one understands it. Smart writers often bristle at the advice that they have to simplify their message and make it more accessible. They resist the idea of "dumbing down" their work.

Often a comedy writer's instinct is to over-complicate their writing, to pack it with deep meaning, esoteric ideas and detailed information.

In *How to Write Funny*, I offered the tip "Keep it Simple." This tip is critical for the single-line joke, but applies to the written piece even more. It's relatively easy to keep a one-line joke simple, but the task of keeping a longer piece simple becomes more difficult with each sentence. Once a reader has plunged into your writing, the water must stay shallow. You can't let them get in over their head. Take your reader by the hand and lead them through your story like a child. Like the first time you read Maurice Sendak's classic, *Where the Wild Things Are*, your reader doesn't know the comedy world you're introducing them to. They need your guidance in order to avoid getting lost or confused.

This is how a great short piece of comedy works: The reader feels as though the writer is taking them on a leisurely stroll along a simple garden path, parasol in hand, and in a careful and measured way, pointing out all the funny and wonderful things in this hilarious comedy world. Showing them too much, or veering off the path by introducing concepts unrelated to your title, or racing through, introducing hard-to-understand concepts too quickly, you'll give the reader more than they bargained for. They'll get scared and abandon the journey.

As the writer, it's your job to give the reader confidence in your ability to lead them along this simple path in a way that's pleasant and reward- ing. Writing a good funny piece has nothing to do with being smart or dumbing down. It's about making your ideas—no matter how brilliant or silly—simple enough for any reader to enjoy.

> FUNNIER-WRITING TIP #10: DON'T COMPLICATE THE IDEA
>
> *Comedy stories are sometimes too dense, have too much going on, or contain too many intricate and complicated attempts by the writer to be clever. Complicating a story is not clever. The trick of good, smart comedy writing is making an astute idea simple enough to appeal to the widest possible audience—from the very smart to the very dumb. Complicating an idea will create something that appeals to no one, because no one will understand it. Remember, people don't put a lot of thought into the information or entertainment they consume. To best entertain them, you need to assume they're taking in your work whimsically and will abandon it at the slightest difficulty. Complicating a piece of writing is the quickest and easiest way to compel a reader to bail on it.*

STRUCTURE

At this stage in the process, you've selected a title, figured out your medium, format and take, and brainstormed joke beats. Now, let's embark on the structure. The take and the structure are closely related. Think of the take as an abstract for your piece, a single sentence describing your approach. For example, in the story, "Man Flattening Cardboard Box Tastes True Power," the take is that everyone, from passersby to the editorial voice to the man himself, accepts the reality that his crushing of the cardboard box gives him a sense of real power. Structure, on the other hand, is more about what Funny Filter is used to achieve the take. In this case, the take will be escalated using the Reference Funny Filter, with details about the man crushing a cardboard box by the trash can in his driveway.

In the next chapter, I'll lay out the 11 different structures you can give your piece using specific examples available for reference online. These

11 structures, based on the Funny Filters, can be mixed, matched, and combined to create countless effective structures to suit the needs of any concept. But in the end, every comedically structured piece has the same simple skeleton: a funny title, followed by a series of escalating joke beats flowing from the title, then a "button" (a closing joke, also called a "closer") at the end.

When writing your first draft (chapter 11), you'll be in Clown mode, embracing everything you write. While you're doing that, try not to second-guess yourself by asking, "Is this simple enough?" That's not the time or place for such a question. The time to keep things simple is where you're at now—after choosing your title and collecting potential joke beats. As you assess those beats, favor the simple ones, the ones that clearly build on the central joke of your title.

Most comedy pieces are written wrong. Most are written with a light, jokey touch, which disregards the "play it straight" tip. Most are written in a stream of consciousness, with randomly constructed jokes that in no way represent the best jokes the writer could have come up with if more time had been spent brainstorming. Frequently, a piece features jokes that have no relation to the title. Jokes often come at the expense of the title, not in support of it. These jokes aren't the result of a culling or vetting process—they're first-draft jokes, and they're almost always subpar. Worse, the piece usually goes off on a tangent. The writer forgets what was funny about the title to begin with, and veers fatally off track. The result? A piece no one can follow and no one wants read.

A comedy piece readers will enjoy—a comedy piece that's funny—is written simply. A great title informs the reader about the joke that'll be told. That joke is then expounded on in the piece through a series of increasingly funny joke beats, starting in the first line, and then continuing every two or three lines throughout the piece. The joke beats escalate the title joke. They build on it and expand it, making it funnier as the piece proceeds, employing the same Funny Filter(s) at work in the title, and often introducing new Funny Filters as the piece escalates. These joke beats serve to fill out the comedy world being presented. The joke beats often occur at the ends of sentences (because the funny part should go last). Between the joke beats are connective tissue: exposition, set up, and other necessary details. As few words as possible are used to communicate the ideas. With each successive line, we know more details about the funny idea introduced in the title. The piece ends with a closer, a joke that wraps up everything with a final laugh. All this is played straight, as if the writer has no idea that the piece is supposed to be funny.

CHAPTER 8 ACTION STEP

Organize the joke beats you brainstormed in the chapter 7 action steps. Weed out any that veer away from the central joke of your title.

LAY YOUR TRACK

When embarking on writing a piece of comedy longer than a single-line joke or gag, you need to figure out how to structure it.

If you're familiar with the craft of dramatic writing, you're certainly familiar with structure. There are voluminous books and courses imparting the complexities of dramatic structure. We'll review dramatic structure and how it applies to comedy writing in chapter 16. Comedically structured writing is different. Whereas dramatic writing is about one action leading to another action, rising tension, climax, and resolution with an emotional investment by the audience, comedic structure is only about joke escalation ending in a button. That's all.

If you're adept at writing drama, you might see comedic structure as a watered-down version of dramatic structure. The inciting incident is the first joke of the piece (which should be communicated in the title), the rising tension is the series of escalating joke beats that follow, each funnier and more heightened than the last, and the resolution is the closer. However, nowhere in comedically structured writing will you find some of the more nuanced steps in dramatic writing, like the "Act II turning point," "descent into the innermost cave," or any of that. You'll almost never use dramatic or emotional hooks, unanswered questions, suspense, or set-ups and pay-offs. Everything is explained up front in comedy, clearly and simply. You also won't find deep, realistic characters, aligned themes, or any serious attempt to engage a range of audience emotions, which are essential to good drama. In comedically structured work, you'll find only one- and two-dimensional characters, Subtext, and jokes.

PUNCHLINES

Punchlines are a little old fashioned but still work for gags. Here's how:

1. There's a set up, where the joke-teller gives the audience all the information they'll need to understand the context of the joke and "get it."

2. There's a slight pause.

3. There's the funny part, or punchline.

Jokes are still told this way, in late-night monologues and other traditional places, but for modern audiences—especially readers of prose, whose attention spans get shorter by the day—such belabored methods of joke telling have fallen out of favor. These days, if you don't have a funny joke in the title of your piece, no one will read it. Nobody's interested in investing the time necessary to read a long, unfunny setup for a punchline. So, prose writers don't necessarily need to think about punchlines. In a modern prose piece, the set up, or exposition, is integrated into the writing, and the punchlines (the joke beats) sneak up on the reader, hitting them with renewed surprise each time.

Another way comedic structure differs from dramatic structure is that it can only sustain an audience's attention for about five minutes. This is enough for a sketch, a scene, a bit, or a short piece of comedy writing. Anything longer needs to use dramatic structure.

The way you determine the best structure for your piece is by looking at the joke of your title and the joke beats you've assembled, and apply the primary Funny Filter of your concept. Together these provide a clue as to the best structure for your piece.

MAINTAINING JOKE DISCIPLINE

Staying on track and only writing jokes that spring from your title is called "joke discipline." This discipline is difficult for a lot of writers to maintain, because after writing a joke they think is funny—regardless of whether it relates to the title—they won't want to cut it, and it invariably brings their piece down. It takes discipline to cut any jokes you come up with—no matter how funny you think they are—and instead go back to the drawing board to generate more jokes that are funny as well as flow logically from the title.

This flow of jokes from the title is like a budding plant, and it's what makes comedic structure. But it only works if the leaves and flowers (the joke beats) are connected to the stem (your title). If they don't spring from your title, that's as incongruent and nonsensical to the reader as elm leaves sprouting from a dandelion stem.

FUNNIER-WRITING TIP #11: STAY ON TRACK

It's easy to veer off course from your core joke. As the writer, you'll get bored with the subject promised by your title and want to liven things up. Or you won't brainstorm enough joke beats that are in line with your take. So, out of desperation, you'll start telling off-take jokes to get what you think will be easier laughs. Don't give in! The best comedy pieces stay on track as diligently as a high-speed train. If you use a joke that doesn't align with the established joke track, the train derails and your readers are lost.

STRUCTURING A PIECE OF COMEDY WRITING

Each of the 11 Funny Filters informs how a comedy piece is structured. Find the structure that fits best with your title and see if the jokes you've brainstormed can stay in line with the title joke when escalated within that structure. Do your jokes tend to heighten the contrast more and more? Then you should structure your piece using Irony. Do your jokes get more absurd? Then use Madcap.

Here are examples of short comedy pieces structured using each of the 11 Funny Filters. Their descriptions are brief, but most of them can be found in their entirety online. Review them to see the structures at work.

IRONY STRUCTURE: The piece builds through the heightening of contrast.

EXAMPLE: The "Black White Supremacist" from *Chappelle's Show* on Comedy Central. In this sketch, we meet blind author Clayton Bigsby. We learn he was raised in an all-white Southern school for the blind and was never told he was black, so he developed into a prominent white supremacist. The first main joke beat of the sketch is Bigsby laying out his racist views of black people (which is ironic coming from a black person). In the next joke beat, he does the same after being confronted by some white racists who don't realize he's a famous Klan leader. This heightens the Irony. The next beat heightens the Irony further when he encounters a group of teens playing rap music. He shouts racist epithets at them, not realizing they're actually white kids who've appropriated black culture and are actually thrilled that someone mistakenly thinks they're black. He then goes to a book signing wearing his Klan hood. The event is packed with his racist white followers. He riles them up with a fiery, racist speech until they demand to see his face, raising the Irony to a fevered pitch. When he reveals his face, a speech attendee's head explodes, adding Shock and Madcap to the Irony.

The sketch lets Parody decide its format, spoofing a profile piece from the PBS series *Frontline*. (The actual *Frontline* announcer narrates it.) The button of the sketch comes in the announcer's closing remarks, saying Bigsby finally came to terms with being white. But then he got divorced, calling his wife a "nigger lover," expertly fusing Irony, Shock, and Parody in the closer.

CHARACTER STRUCTURE: The piece builds through a character acting on their traits under increasingly heightened circumstances.

EXAMPLE: Simon Rich's "Math Problems," from *Ant Farm*. It's a short parody of a high-school test with math problems, and the character is the teacher. In the first test question (the first joke beat), the teacher compares the cost of name-brand rum to generic rum and asks students to calculate how much he'll save over different years. This establishes the take that the teacher will inappropriately reveal details of his sad life in the math problems. The next beat asks students to do some math to calculate the square footage of the teacher's new studio apartment. In the next problem, the math concerns the distance, in feet, that the teacher must legally keep away from his ex-wife. The comedy world of this story and its character escalate by becoming more pathetic the more we learn about the teacher. His character is drawn through these beats: he's a depressed divorcée whose life is falling apart. The Subtext comes through the key word (with a double meaning) in the title: "problems." Yes, this teacher has many problems. The button of the piece is when he reveals his emotions: "How many hours a day is he frightened? What is he so afraid of?"

REFERENCE STRUCTURE: The piece deepens its relatability.

EXAMPLE: Tom Hanks' opening monologue from *SNL*, October 22, 2016. Hanks explains that a magazine recently called him "America's Dad." He changes into a sweater, the lights dim, and he has a father-son talk with the nation. He addresses us as, "buddy," "champ," and "kiddo." He talks about how we've had a rough year, how we're anxious, and that maybe we're just in an awkward phase. Everything he says is recognizable from what a real dad says in such talks, and all his mannerisms and tone reference the way the typical dad behaves in these circumstances. The situation becomes more and more relatable with each successive beat.

The monologue also employs Analogy structure, analogizing America with a child.

SHOCK STRUCTURE: The piece gets more shocking by employing increasingly innovative Shock.

EXAMPLE: The Mr. Creosote sketch from Monty Python's *The Meaning of Life*. An impossibly fat man, Mr. Creosote, waddles into a fancy French restaurant. This is the first beat of very mild gross-out humor. Each beat gets progressively more gross, with Mr. Creosote swearing at the waiter, and then repeatedly projectile vomiting into a bucket and then on top of a cleaning woman sent over to wash up the vomit that missed the bucket. The Shock only gets more disgusting from there, and it's all in service of great Subtext: the over-consumption of the world's privileged classes is disgusting. Note how the Funny Filter used for this sketch serves as a symbol for the Subtext: it's disgusting how the world's elites consume more than their fair share of resources, so Monty Python uses disgusting gross-out humor. The joke beats of the sketch escalate until Mr. Creosote explodes from eating too much, drenching everyone in the restaurant with his innards. As everyone bellows in disgust and the place is reduced to bedlam, the waiter, John Cleese, daintily delivers the check to Mr. Creosote. That's the button of the sketch.

HYPERBOLE STRUCTURE: the piece becomes more exaggerated.

EXAMPLE: Patton Oswalt's bit about the prescription drug epidemic in his *Talking for Clapping* stand-up special. Oswalt uses hyperbole a lot, as do many stand-up comedians. But very few can use it to structure a bit the way Oswalt can. Hyperbole is one of the most difficult structures to use because it starts with exaggeration beyond reality, so the writer is faced with the daunting challenge of escalating it even further beyond reality. Oswalt starts with a simple story of his doctor prescribing Ambien. Then his mother offers him Ambien after a flight, with a pill bottle "the size of a police flashlight." He tells a story of her doctor offering her an M&M's candy cane full of sedatives. He escalates to the sound of a truck backing up, dumping pills, then to the idea of the doctor offering his mother a scoop and sending her to the "bulk section." After that, he says seniors are invited to a "pill party" that would bring Bob Fosse back to life and then kill him again." He says that lost inside your parents couch cushions is another Coachella.

PARODY STRUCTURE: The verisimilitude heightens.

EXAMPLE: "Professor Richard Dawkins Speaks at Fair Hills Kindergarten Regarding Santa Claus," by Mike Jones, published in *McSweeney's*. Famous atheist and scientist Richard Dawkins' patterns of speech and agnosticism are parodied in this sober chat with kindergarteners. The verisimilitude is so spot-on, you can almost hear Dawkins reading the piece aloud. The joke beats are nearly continuous. They escalate both the joke (that he is destroying the magic of Christmas for these children) and the excellent Subtext, which is widely accessible because it changes depending on where you stand on the religious spectrum. (If you agree with Dawkins, the Subtext is that a belief in God is as silly as a belief in Santa Claus; but if you don't agree with him, the Subtext is that Dawkins is a buzzkill, taking joy and meaning from those empowered by their beliefs.) The continued aping of Richard Dawkins' talking points and recognizable phrases, as well as the way he structures an argument, become the structure of the piece.

WORDPLAY STRUCTURE: The piece offers up more and more wordplay.

EXAMPLE: "Earthquake Marks Least Gay Day in San Francisco History," from *The Onion*'s *Our Dumb Century*. With the subheads, "'Queen City on the Pacific' Lies in Ruins," and 'Garment District Still Flaming," this piece uses a series of double entendres, referring to both the 1906 earthquake and words commonly associated with gay culture. An added lack of awareness from the anachronism brings out rich Subtext, elevating the piece to more than just a string of gay puns. The format is a newspaper story, but the structure of the piece is successively inventive and ridiculous wordplay, building the dramatic irony and anachronistic tension more and more as it goes on.

ANALOGY STRUCTURE: The piece finds more connections between the two halves of the analogy.

EXAMPLE: "Al Gore Places Infant Son In Rocket To Escape Dying Planet," from *The Onion*. Analogy is one of the most common structures used in short comedy pieces because it's simple to understand. The joke beats come whenever the hidden half of the analogy is mapped on top of the overt half, making a connection. In this story, Al Gore is compared with Superman's father on the planet Krypton, Jor-El. (Gore is called "Go-re-Al" later in the piece, a wonderful bit of Wordplay mapping.) Krypton's imminent destruction is mapped onto climate change. The analogy is rich with comparisons between the two disparate subjects, and each new comparison is expertly mapped to make for a clear succession of joke beats that build to greater drama, evoking the epic story of Superman's flight from his dying home planet.

MADCAP STRUCTURE: See how much sillier you can make it.

EXAMPLE: *LiarTownUSA*, by Sean Tejaratchi, is a treasure-trove of original and delightful Madcap, Shock, Wordplay and especially Parody. Parodies of strange and random publications or screenshots populate his blog and are collected in his book, *LiarTown: The First Four Years*. One series of "Craft and DYI Publications" uses Madcap as the primary Funny Filter, starting with a book called *Sweet Potato Dolls*, which features photos of random people's faces stapled onto sweet potatoes. He escalates the joke by making each successive publication (each joke beat) progressively sillier. The next is *Rumanian Punishment Gifts*, which features sad-looking dolls that appear to be made from wrinkled, spoiled onions. Later is *Make-It-Yourself Fuckable Easter Fleshlight*, with a Fleshlight on the cover adorned like a fancy Easter egg. Then comes several publications featuring an imagined crafts trend called "Antique Wooden Cussin' Bears," cute woodcut bears holding signs that say "fuck you," "get fucked," and "balls." An excellent technique for escalating on any joke track is to introduce other Funny Filters (in this case, Shock) to amp up the laughs, yet maintain joke discipline by remaining on the same joke track (in this case, funny craft publications).

MISPLACED FOCUS STRUCTURE: The writer gets closer to the elephant in the room without acknowledging it.

EXAMPLE: "A Modest Proposal," by Jonathan Swift. This classic work of satire uses Misplaced Focus to structure its joke beats. In the essay, Swift proposes addressing the problem of poor children in Ireland by eating them. Every joke beat drills in with more focused detail on the eating: how to prepare, cook, and distribute the children as food. All the while he ignores the real issue (that these children are victims of economic injustice), building and escalating the tension with each sentence.

METAHUMOR STRUCTURE: The piece deepens its critique of the humor in question.

EXAMPLE: The "Bawdy 70s Hospital" sketch from BBC's *That Mitchell and Webb Look*. This sketch features a parody of an innuendo-laden hospital-based TV show in the 70s, filled with clichéd puns like a doctor telling a patient before giving him a shot, "You'll feel a little prick," and the patient responding, "It wouldn't be the first," and a nurse offering tea or coffee in two different pitchers to a patient who says, "That's a lovely pair of jugs." Everyone plays along, tongue in cheek, until the game of the scene is introduced. The joke beats on this track come from a doctor who doesn't understand innuendo humor. He hears all the sexually suggestive banter and asks, as if he's starting to get aroused, "Shall I get my cock out?" The sketch beats escalate perfectly, with two awkward interruptions of dialog by the doctor, the second more explicit than the first. Then he's taken into the hospital administrator's office where he admits he can't tell the difference between double entendre and on-the-nose dialog. The humor of such bawdy shows is then deconstructed and explained dispassionately by the administrator. The button for the sketch comes when the administrator asks the doctor to leave through the "rear entrance." The doctor, now having learned what the show is supposed to be about, awkwardly tries to play along by saying, "Ooh oh missus?" but it's too little too late, and the administrator doesn't find his lackluster response funny.

For a final example, let's check back in with Robert's cardboard-box story: His title uses Character and Reference primarily, and most of the riffs he got from his feedback group that resonated with him were escalations of both Reference and Character, exploring more nuanced and relatable aspects of what it's like to breakdown a cardboard box, and drilling deeper into who the Character was and showing him acting on his traits. So he chose to structure his piece using a combination of Reference and Character.

If you're stuck with no clear way to structure your piece, let these examples show you the possibilities. There are countless ways to format a piece, but only 11 ways to structure it. Simply select a Funny Filter that aligns with your title so that all your joke beats make sense within the story, build, and get funnier. You can also combine the 11 structures in creative ways, like Robert and some of the others did, just like you can combine the Funny Filters in a joke. But for now I recommend sticking with one primary Funny Filter per piece for your structure to keep things simple.

The more you write, the more you'll tend to favor certain Funny Filters. This, coupled with the formats you use, will help define your unique voice as a writer.

CHAPTER 9 ACTION STEPS

1. Explore what kinds of structures might work with your comedy piece. Go through each of the 11 Funny Filter-inspired structures and imagine how your piece will play out.

2. Choose the best structure for your piece. Know it may change if you discover a better take after drafting, and that's okay. Use the best one you can come up with now in order to move forward.

ESCALATE

Jokes must get bigger and better in your comedy piece. They must escalate. If they don't, you're either repeating the same joke over and over, or worse, you're getting off track with jokes that aren't in line with your take.

Professional short comedy escalates. And the best short comedy escalates at an optimal pace. You've probably seen sketches toward the end of *SNL* where the joke of the scene is established but then seems to take too long to get to the second joke beat. This happens when a piece escalates too slowly, and it makes for a boring sketch. This is common in comedy written by beginners.

It's rare that a short piece of comedy escalates too quickly. In such a piece, the audience won't be bored; they'll merely be racing to keep up with it. This often happens with intermediate writers, who, having figured out how to use joke beats, feel like they can maximize the comedic punch of their concept by cramming joke beats too closely together. Or they're afraid of losing their audience's attention so they don't want too much dead space between joke beats.

Ideally, you want to find the sweet spot in the middle: a comfortable, confident pace that's not too slow and not too fast.

Parody news stories in *The Onion* usually offer a good example of well-paced escalating joke beats. Those in *Blaffo*, the other humor magazine I founded, certainly do. The stories in Simon Rich's *Ant Farm* are another good example of well-paced escalation.

Aside from pacing your joke beats properly, you also need to manage how much they escalate, regardless of the pace.

Portlandia has some of the best joke-beat escalation in short comedy. Their sketches serve as a model for every comedy writer who wonders whether their joke beats are escalating too much or too soon. The writers of *Portlandia* escalate at a nice pace. It's fast, but not too fast. But where the show excels is in how much it escalates. They know audiences instinctively understand the short-comedy genre and anticipate the standard range of joke escalation in sketches, but they turn it up higher than anyone has since *Monty Python*. Each joke beat takes a nice leap, and jokes never repeat or escalate marginally like they can in other sketches.

Portlandia's "Colin the Chicken / Aliki Farms" sketch, for example, starts as a standard restaurant sketch, like a thousand others we've seen on TV. The characters, played by Fred Armisen and Carrie Brownstein, are introduced as overly concerned about how responsibly the chicken on the menu was farmed, asking about the chicken's diet and how organic it was. The sketch quickly escalates to the waitress telling them what the chicken's name was, showing them a photo and his papers.

That's as far as most sketches would probably go. But *Portlandia* keeps escalating, going further than the audience can imagine. The diners ask about the farmers who raised the chicken and how genuine they are. They decide to leave the restaurant and visit the farm to make sure it's a responsible choice. There they meet demure, glaze-eyed women in long skirts lovingly scattering feed for the free-range chickens. They also meet Aliki, the leader of the farm, played by Jason Sudeikis. He mesmerizes the diners with his charisma and they fall in love with the idyllic community, joining it for life, and becoming members of a polygamous cult as well as Aliki's newest wives.

That's some serious escalation.

> FUNNIER-WRITING TIP #12: INTEGRATE EXPOSITION
>
> *Don't spend a lot of time explaining the logic of your piece. Just make it funny and fold any essential information into the joke beats so readers don't realize they're having things explained to them humorlessly. In old-style humor, long setups were used to set the stage for a joke, and then the funny part would come last in the form of a punchline. But now, especially in prose, it's best to integrate any long and potentially boring explanations or setups so the reader can get to the funny part as quickly as possible.*

Most comedy pieces don't escalate enough. Amateur writers, especially, don't escalate far. They often think the joke beats are escalating, but they're not; they're escalating too subtly for the reader to notice. You can almost always escalate more than you think. Just make sure each joke beat is logically connected to the last so the audience isn't left behind. You need to pull them along with you, never allowing them to predict where you're going, but always making sure they're with you.

This is the goal of your piece. If you can escalate your title joke by creating increasingly funny joke beats on the same subject and in the same world—on the same track—then your piece has a good chance of working. Escalating is one of the most difficult things to do in comedy writing, and it's where the real heavy lifting is done.

One reason escalation is difficult is that you have to invent new jokes, and each one has to be bigger and better than the last. Your feedback group can certainly help you with riffing, and if they do a spectacular job you may only need to lay out their joke beats. But in the final stretch, it will always come down to you, the lone writer, putting the words together and making the joke beats work.

To see escalation at work, let's break down the "Substitute Teacher" sketch from *Key & Peele*. It has millions of views on YouTube and is one of their most successful sketches. It's a textbook example of well-placed—and well paced—escalating joke beats.

The perfectly structured sketch uses almost all the 11 Funny Filters as well as relevant and meaty Subtext. (The Subtext of the sketch is that it's frustrating that black and white cultures don't understand each other.) Before breaking down the escalation in the sketch, let's look at the wealth of Funny Filters at work:

• Character: Mr. Garvey is an archetype (the tough inner-city school-teacher), and in order to create laughs, they show him acting on the standard traits of this archetype (that he's black-identified, tough, and doesn't take any shit).

• Irony: Placing a black inner-city schoolteacher in an evidently well-funded all-white classroom creates nice, extreme contrast.

• Misplaced focus: Mr. Garvey's intense focus on the wrong thing (the incorrect pronunciations of names), ignores the elephant in the room (the clash of races).

• Wordplay: The way names are pronounced is textbook Wordplay.

• Reference: We've all experienced the awkward substitute teacher who can't connect with the class.

• Hyperbole: Mr. Garvey uses impossible exaggeration (like "break my foot off in your ass" and others) when he threatens the kids.

• Parody: The sketch loosely parodies movies like *Stand and Deliver* and *Lean On Me*, about tough, inner-city teachers or principals whipping a school or classroom into shape.

• Shock: There's plenty of mild Shock with great Subtext in this sketch, like Mr. Garvey's swearing, his threats of violence, the diagram of sex organs on the blackboard, and the racial tension.

• Madcap: Mr. Garvey's heightening physicality counts as Madcap.

• Metahumor: There's a subtle moment where a student laughs at what Mr. Garvey's doing. It's a nice little garnish of metahumor that deepens the verisimilitude.

With all these Funny Filters and great Subtext, the writers of this sketch set themselves up with a cornucopia of tools to brainstorm great joke beats and escalate those beats masterfully.

Here are the joke beats of the sketch broken down:

INTRODUCTION: The first beat is not a joke. It's expository, simply to explain the scenario as clearly as possible. Mr. Garvey enters the classroom and explains he's from the inner-city and therefore tough. By showing him facing a crowd of all-white students, the writers establish the situation, his archetype, and the Irony.

This sketch can afford to violate Funnier-Writing Tip #12, ("Integrate Exposition," page 92). It does its best to integrate the exposition, using the introduction to lay out as much information about the character and situation as needed to understand the game of the scene to come. In prose, you can't afford this because your first joke beat must be in the title of your piece in order to get readers' attention and compel them to read further. An online video needs a funny title for the same reason. But if you're a successful show on Comedy Central like *Key & Peele*, you don't need any of that. They already have their audience's attention, and their viewers will grant them a few seconds at the beginning of a sketch because they trust *Key & Peele* to deliver the comedy.

JOKE BEAT ONE: Taking attendance, Mr. Garvey asks for "J-Quellen." No one answers until a girl tentatively raises her hand and says, nonplussed, "Do you mean Jacqueline?"

The funniest part of the beat (naturally, the last part) is Mr. Garvey's reaction. His blood boils from the racial tension but he tries to keep his cool. He sets down his clipboard, puts his fists on the table, and says, "Okay, so that's how it's gonna be. Y'all wanna play?" And then he threatens her as if the game is on: "I got my eye on you, J-Quellen," he says, pointing.

This beat escalates both his anger and the Funny Filters at play. It does this by adding Wordplay to the previous mix of Character, Parody, and Irony established in the introduction. After this joke beat, we know the take—the game of the scene: this sketch will be about him mispronouncing white names to be more "black."

Joke beats come in different shapes and sizes. Every piece of comedy will be different depending on the needs of the concept. The joke beats in this sketch are three-parters. Each one features a setup (Mr. Garvey calling out the name), a payoff (the student responding to the name), and then a reaction (Mr. Garvey getting angry). It's a simple, easy-to-follow structure that comes with at least three different ways for the writers to escalate each beat.

the short comedy piece

button

joke beat

joke beat

joke beat

joke beat

joke beat

joke beat

title

JOKE BEAT TWO: Mr. Garvey asks for "B'lockay." Here it may feel like the same joke is being told: it's another mispronounced white name to sound black. But even the first part of this beat (the setup) is an escalation of the previous beat because the audience is now engaged in a guessing game for a moment, trying to figure out what white name Mr. Garvey is mispronouncing this time.

Then, with the payoff, a student raises his hand and says, slightly less sheepishly than Jacqueline, but still somewhat intimidated by Mr. Garvey, "My name's Blake." This time, instead of giving the teacher the benefit of the doubt like Jacqueline did, Blake states his name's correct pronunciation as a fact, not a question. This escalates the conflict.

The reaction, which the audience now expects, is delivered in a surprising way, with Mr. Garvey first asking incredulously, "Are you out of your goddamned mind?" He then mocks Blake by imitating the way he said his name: "Blaaake." This escalates by introducing Shock and another layer of Parody (parodying the way Blake speaks). Finally, he shows his true anger by raising his voice to a new, funnier pitch, pointing at Blake angrily and yelling, "Do you want to go to war, B'lockay?" They have a tense exchange, escalating the pace of the dialog, ending with Mr. Garvey promising, "I'm for real. *I'm for real!* So you better check yourself!" Blake is confused but also a little scared, escalating the tension further.

JOKE BEAT THREE: Mr. Garvey looks at his clipboard and calls out the next name: "Dee-nice." A girl who knows he's referring to her sits in silence, refusing at first to play his game, escalating the tension. Mr. Garvey says the name again, and then breaks the joke-beat pattern slightly (another escalation) by revealing his anger in advance of the next student speaking up: "If one of y'all says some silly-ass name, this whole class is gonna feel my wrath!"

After he impatiently calls the name a third time, the girl relents, saying, "You mean Denise?" but in a more dismissive way than the previous two students, escalating the conflict.

In part three of the beat, Mr. Garvey breaks his clipboard in half over his knee, escalating the physicality (Madcap). "Son of a bitch!" he yells. Denise flinches, escalating the tension. Mr. Garvey then demands she say her name "right," and they have an intense and repeated back and forth, more intense than with Blake:

"Say it right."

"Denise."

"Correctly."

"Denise."

"Right."

"Denise."

This escalates the conflict to a new peak, making the audience wonder who will give in. Denise loses the battle, finally throwing up her hands: "Dee-nice?" Mr. Garvey is pleased and relieved.

JOKE BEAT FOUR: Mr. Garvey picks up his now broken clipboard, escalating the Irony of the scene, and calls out a new name: "A-A-ron." This is an even more ridiculous mispronunciation than the previous names, escalating the Madcap and Wordplay. He calls for the student several times with variations in delivery, escalating the tension. We see the student who is presumably Aaron sitting silently and shaking his head, refusing to answer, escalating the conflict further than Denise.

"Well you better be sick, dead, or mute, A-A-ron," Mr. Garvey says. This veiled threat finally compels Aaron to eek out a quick "Here," followed by, "Oh man," under his breath, escalating the conflict and tension further.

The joke beat is prolonged when Mr. Garvey walks up to Aaron, gets in his face, and asks him why he didn't answer. When Aaron admits he didn't answer because his name is pronounced "Aaron," Mr. Garvey swears again and, in a rage, sweeps everything off his table onto the floor, escalating his Character, the Madcap, and the tension to a new pitch.

JOKE BEAT FIVE: Mr. Garvey yells at Aaron at the top of his voice and orders him to go to "O'Shag-Hennesy's office." Aaron asks, "Who?" and Mr. Garvey yells the name again. Aaron asks, "Principal O'Shaughnessy?" At this, Mr. Garvey screams and swears at Aaron as he expels him from the class.

This joke beat escalates by broadening the comedy world created by the sketch. In this world, the one impossible thing is a black teacher who doesn't know how to pronounce white names. The sketch shows its joke discipline despite the fevered pitch of emotions at play, staying on track with only jokes about Mr. Garvey mispronouncing white names, never about anything else. But with this beat the writers asked, "If this is true, what else is true?" And they realized that if Mr. Garvey gets students' names wrong, he probably gets other people's names wrong too. The absurdity of the funny situation is consistent with the laws of this world. Of course in reality he would run into myriad problems mispronouncing names like this, especially when it comes to his boss, the principal. But in this illogical comedy world, the one thing that's off (Mr. Garvey's mispronunciation of white names) has to be consistent, no matter how illogical it would be in the real world.

JOKE BEAT SIX (THE CLOSER):

In this simple beat, Mr. Garvey reads one more name, "Tim—O-thee." A lone black student peers out from behind someone in the back row, raises his hand and says, "Present," pronouncing it "PREE-zent." Mr. Garvey, in exasperated relief, puts a nice button on the sketch with an emphatic, "Thank you!"

This beat flips the joke upside-down, showing the situation from a black perspective, where names—and even other words—are pronounced the way Mr. Garvey expects.

FUNNIER-WRITING TIP #13: RESPECT INTERNAL LOGIC

When creating a comedy world, which happens every time you have a funny title or concept, you need to know the rules of the world. In a comedy piece, it's a world that's slightly askew from the real world with one impossible thing that makes it different. Don't break the rules of your comedy world. Don't create two different jokes that clash and are impossible within the same set of rules. Changing the rules arbitrarily confuses your readers and compels them to give up on your piece. Sometimes the rules will concern the nature of reality or the way characters in your piece behave. Other times the rules will concern you, and how you address the reader. Don't break character as a narrator or editorial voice, and don't ever reveal your awareness that there's something off about this world. In order to play it straight, either you or key characters (or both) must pretend everything in this crazy comedy world you've created is perfectly normal and consistent.

It's worth noting that escalating anger and tension works well in a performed sketch, where characters can play the anger straight, as Keegan-Michael Key does in "Substitute Teacher." But these kinds of outbursts often don't work in prose. Unhinged behavior comes off as the writer failing to play it straight.

The joke beats in this sketch are rather long and contain separate parts. Joke beats in other sketches may be shorter. For example, joke beats in a written piece may be just a few words at the ends of sentences. Every piece is different, but they all have the same skeleton: a joke is established, then escalated through joke beats, then finished with a button.

THE CLOSER

The last joke of a short comedy piece is the closer. Some call it a button. After building your joke beats up to be crazier and crazier but staying carefully on track, you now have a chance to do something slightly different.

The closer joke is the one time you're allowed to veer slightly off-take if you want. This joke should be different in some way than all the others. It can be the opposite of all your previous jokes, as it is in "Substitute Teacher." It can nullify everything that came before it and possibly even destroy the internal logic of the piece. If it's funny, there's no reason not to take the whole world down with you. The piece is over, so why not have fun? Like with any joke, you can brainstorm closers using the Divining method. There you'll find possibilities that can work with your particular concept.

In a recent story by Constantine Platanias for *Blaffo*, the closer uses a powerful Reference joke with its own strong Subtext that's different than the Subtext of the piece. The piece was "More Busy Executives Are Saving Time by Shitting in Their Pants Standing Up." The Subtext of the story is corporate executives, like babies, are over-privileged. Each joke beat concerns scenarios in which specific business leaders shat in their pants at work. The closer: "While CEOs are credited with popularizing the trend, it isn't just for those at the top of the corporate ladder. According to Amazon Warehouse Associate Dean Haldegeld, 'I've been shitting on the job for years.'" The knowing reference to an actual current event in the real world (Amazon warehouse workers not being allowed adequate bathroom breaks) made for a nice way to end the piece.

How your closer works will depend on the particular Funny Filters and Subtext of your piece. In a Misplaced Focus joke, sometimes a closer works when the elephant in the room is blatantly identified. If your piece uses no Irony, sometimes the sudden introduction of Irony can make a good closer. There are countless variations to try.

The only requirement of a closer is that it must feel like an ending, not just another beat in the piece like all the others. It should wrap up the piece in some way, put a cap on it, and leave the audience remembering it fondly.

CHAPTER 10 ACTION STEP

Sort your best joke-beat ideas, ranking them from the most basic to the most crazy, from the funny to the funniest, capping the list with your best closer joke. This list will serve as the outline for your first draft.

SPIT OUT A DRAFT

This chapter is not a checklist for you to reference while you write your rough draft. Read it before you write your draft, then put the book down, do your best to internalize the advice, and then just start writing. Finish your draft in less than 30 minutes.

Think of this initial draft like a glorified Morning Pages exercise. Just move your fingers. Refer to your joke beat outline you made in the chapter 10 Actions Steps—that's your cheat sheet. Put the beats where they belong, and compile the connective tissue between the joke beats in a way that's good enough. Don't sweat it. Don't obsess over every word. Don't erase and go back. Rush through this draft and just get to the end. Don't ask yourself whether it's any good. That doesn't matter right now. What matters is getting it written.

The instinct of most writers at this stage is to carefully craft their first draft, pouring over the construction of every sentence. This is a trap and will lead to frustration. Instead, move forward with abandon, trust your concept, and trust this process. The time for carefully selecting every word and minding every detail to make the writing "perfect" is later.

You've laid the groundwork for a good piece of writing. Your concept, like a foundation for a new house, is solid. The concrete is laid and smoothed out in your basement. You're nowhere near ready to start putting up drapes. What you're ready to do is unload two-by-four studs and two-by-six joists from a truck and stack them at the construction site. Actually nailing them together into a frame comes next.

Just like you wouldn't show off an unfinished house to impress any neighbors just yet (in fact, you're best off hiding your lumber under tarps to protect it from rain, maybe even putting a fence around the site so it's not an eyesore in the neighborhood), don't show this rough draft to anybody.

"it's hilarious!"

Nobody starts out great. It takes practice to get good at anything. On a macro level, it takes practice to get good at writing short comedy pieces. On a micro level, it takes practice to get good at writing the particular story you're writing now. You've never written this piece before, so your rough draft is probably not going to be very good. It's certainly not going to dazzle anyone, least of all yourself. That's okay. Don't crumple any drafts and throw them in the trash (this is another wrong-headed cliché of writing you see in pop culture all the time). You must embrace this messy step as part of the process, a necessary component of an excellent final result, no different than when you wrote a lot of bad titles to arrive at your good one.

Below is the rough draft Robert wrote for his cardboard-box story. Note the many errors and loose structure. He moved forward without concern for these things, without judging the piece. He knew the important thing at this stage was simply to get it written.

MAN FLATTENING CARDBOARD BOX TASTES TRUE POWER

Flattening some cardboard boxes, local pharmacy worker Richard Nelson tasted true power. According to neighbors, Nelson, a divorced father of two, spent the first moments of his Tuesday evening summoning strength to flatten the cardboard boxes he used to move into his new studio apartment. Hmmpf! One. Hmmpf! Two! Yeah! Three! C'mon, who wants some? Four. He ripped apart a lot of boxes with his bare hands, smashed the, with the force of a man half his age. Soon after crushing the cardboard into swares, Nelson reportedly got a brief wiff of what it means to have real might. 'To be honest, I thought I would just head in early, or maybe just grab a beer and watch TV. If I'd known that kind of power was inside me, I probably would have flattened those suckers weeks ago," said Nelson while making a sigh and clutching his biceps. After a 10 hour workday and eating a microwave frozen food, Nelson believed to be ordering items he didn't need on Amazon in hopes of chasing the fleeting feeling.

Make your draft around the same length as Robert's. The longer your article, the more difficult it will be to sustain with comedic structure. Starting small like this, with no more than a half page or about 200–500 words, will make this step less stressful. When you've written a few pieces and you're comfortable with that length, try to go longer, up to 1,000 or 1,500 words. If you go any longer, you're straining readers' tolerance for a short comedy piece. However, in a first draft, writing long is okay. You can always cull it down later.

Note how Robert puts his title at the top of his piece. This is extremely important. Your title is the first beat of your joke. It's what introduces readers to your piece and compels them to read it. No one is ever going to read a block of copy with no context. Your title is like the front door of your house; without one, no one can get in.

FUNNIER-WRITING TIP #14: DON'T REVEAL YOUR SUBTEXT

If you have astute Subtext in your piece, it will elevate your work to the level of Satire, which makes your material more accessible and therefore more successful. When you have good Subtext, you may be tempted to spell it out directly in your piece, saying it "on the nose." For example, if your Subtext is, "Snails are gross," don't write, "I looked at a snail and thought, 'ooh, gross.'" You must never do this. If you do, your piece will fall apart. And be careful—Subtext may sneak in without your noticing, disguised as a quote from a character in your piece. Instead, use the timeless writing advice, "Show, Don't Tell": make a joke about how a snail has pizza sauce all over its mouth, hasn't showered in days, and is just chilling and watching porn. Subtext is meant to be hidden. Your job as a comedy writer is to tell jokes that make your reader come up with the Subtext on their own but never see it overtly.

After you write your rough draft, do something else. Go out with friends, watch a movie, go through the motions at your nine-to-five job for a few days—anything other than tinkering with your draft.

If you're obsessed with writing and have already made it a daily habit, by all means keep writing every day, but work on a different piece, or different projects. Try not to think about the particular rough draft you just wrote.

Get out of your head and into the world. Live your life. At this stage, these are the most helpful things you can do for the future quality of your piece.

After this rest period, come back to your rough draft and clean it up as much as you need to make it understandable to a reader. This is easier after you've had some time way from it. You might have enough distance to perceive the piece as a reader would. You'll see its flaws more clearly. Fix typos, correct spelling, and rearrange sentences if necessary. Technically speaking, this will be your first draft. The rough draft doesn't count because no one will ever see it. Before you show anything to anyone—even your feedback groups—you want to edit it and proof it and make sure it's presentable and makes sense. Your rough draft probably won't meet this standard, but this slightly more polished first draft will. Don't edit your first draft too much during this pass. Just clean it up and make sure the joke beats are where you want them, and make sure the piece works as well as you can make it without straining yourself.

After forgetting about his draft for a while, Robert returned to it and cleaned it up. Here's what his first draft looked like:

MAN FLATTENING CARDBOARD BOX TASTES TRUE POWER

WORCESTER, MA—Following a thorough flattening of some cardboard boxes, local pharmacy technician Richard Nelson tasted true power. According to neighbors, Nelson, 54, a divorced father of two, was said to have spent the waning moments of his Tuesday evening summoning the strength to flatten the cardboard boxes he had used to move into his new studio apartment. "Hmmpf! One. Hmmpf! Two! Yeah! Three! C'mon, who wants some? Four," Nelson growled, ripping apart box after box apart with his bare hands, pancaking the strewn cardboard remnants with the force of a man half his age and with twice his command. Soon after crushing the cardboard into flattened squares, Nelson reportedly received a brief and heady waft of what it means to possess real might. "To be honest, I thought I would just head in early, or maybe just grab a beer and watch TV. If I'd known that kind of power was inside me, I probably would have flattened those suckers weeks ago," said Nelson while emitting a brief sigh and clutching his biceps. After a 10-hour workday and eating a microwavable frozen meal, Nelson was believed to be ordering items he didn't otherwise need on Amazon.com in hopes of chasing the fleeting feeling.

Robert's piece is still rough, but in the next few steps, it will be improved. What matters is he wrote it.

> **FUNNIER-WRITING TIP #15: DON'T EXPLAIN YOUR FUNNY SITUATION WITH LOGIC**
>
> *When writing a humor piece, some writers make the mistake of explaining why their funny world makes sense according to the rules of the real world, or how it all works based on real-world logic. Don't ever do this. That's akin to revealing your Subtext. A comedy world should be illogical. There is something askew about it—your one impossible thing. As the writer, your job is merely to show us this crazy world, not tell us why or how it's possible. Treat it like it makes perfect logical sense even though it's inherently illogical. This is a key ingredient to making humor come off as funny. Once you explain it, you dismantle the humor. This tip is distinct from the earlier tip, (#13: "Respect Internal Logic"). The internal logic of your comedy world is important to respect; real-world logic should never be applied to your piece to make sense of it. Respect the illogic of your comedy world as if it's logical.*

CHAPTER 11 ACTION STEPS

1. Write a rough draft according to the outline of joke beats you compiled in the chapter 10 Action Step.

2. Forget about your rough draft for a few days.

3. Make any edits necessary to shape your rough draft into a first draft that's accessible and understandable.

YOUR WRITING PROCESS

You've probably been writing comedy for a while now. You've written jokes, joke beats, and Morning Pages. But if the Action Step in the last chapter was your first experience writing a paragraph or two of funny prose, it may feel like you've taken a quantum leap. You may feel like you're a real, actual writer now.

You are!

So far we've been talking about the process of writing a short comedy piece. But when other writers talk about a "writing process," they mean something else. They mean the conditions they prefer for writing—their routine and habits.

A lot of beginning writers want to know what a good writing process is. Where should you write? How should you write? What process has worked for other writers to get in the mood or find inspiration?

Let's take a breather from our writing-a-short-piece process to look at the idea of a general writing process.

Writing is hard, especially when you haven't done it much. Most writers find not writing to be a lot easier than writing. While writing, they'll allow themselves to get distracted by just about anything, from texting to email to scrubbing the bathtub—anything to avoid writing. It takes a lot of discipline to break through the psychological barriers and sit down and put words on pages. By trying, you're fighting against your powerful mammalian need for instant gratification, forcing yourself to do something that's painful in the moment yet pleasurable in the long term, which is one of the most difficult things to do in life.

writing process

Most writers agree, motivating yourself is difficult. So they come up with processes. They collect comforts and prompts that pump them up to do the hard work of writing. Some writers like to be in a certain cozy place, write at a certain time of day when no one will bother them, have a certain beverage at hand, or play certain music. All of this is fine, and you should adopt whatever accouterments work best for you. There's no right or wrong process as long as it gets you writing.

There's only one component of process that matters: making writing a regular habit. Writers write; non-writers put off writing. According to the latest science, if you do the same thing for about 30 days straight, it will become a habit. Once writing is a habit, you won't need motivation or a process in order to start writing. You'll find yourself writing before you even know what you're doing. And that's where a successful and prolific writer needs to be.

One way to develop a habit is spelled out in *How to Write Funny*: do the Morning Pages exercise until you can't stop the avalanche of writing that'll pour out of you. Get more out of the exercise by continuing it, day after day.

If you're starting out and you don't have any momentum, getting a writing habit started is difficult. There are a few things that can help:

1. Create a trigger. Eat a certain stack or drink, or smell a certain smell. Make a certain gesture or say a certain phrase. Are you a visual learner, an auditory learner, or a kinesthetic learner? Use a trigger most effective for your preferred learning style. Whatever trigger you concoct, do it every time you begin to write. This will help train your brain to associate this simple trigger to writing, and over time it will take less work to gear you up. Eventually, you'll be able to simply use your trigger to get yourself writing, quickly and automatically.

2. Establish a routine. Do your writing at the same time and, if possible, in the same place every day. This conditions your brain to accept the new habit by creating a slew of sensory associations with the new activity and committing it to your brain's list of rote processes.

3. Reward yourself after you write. Once you've written for an hour or two, or whatever time span you've chosen, do something you love doing. Eat a treat, enjoy some entertainment, relax—whatever guilty or not-so-guilty pleasure you enjoy. This will further condition your brain to find the writing process pleasurable, and work in tandem with the trigger and the routine to make you the kind of writer you want to be. But whatever you do, don't partake of this reward before you write, or fail to sit still and write for the duration. Make it a special reward you only get for sitting down and putting words on pages for the specified time frame you've chosen. You don't give a dog a treat if he doesn't roll over like you asked, so don't give yourself a treat before you've done your writing. If you do, your brain will get confused, you won't learn the subconscious discipline you need, and pretty soon you'll be peeing on the carpet.

If you think you might be tempted by distraction, turn off your phone and disconnect your Internet while you write.

Another technique you can use to keep your mind on writing is to set an alarm before you write. If you plan to write for a set amount of time, an alarm does a great job of sharpening your focus, keeping you on task, and reminding you of the value of the time.

On a more surface level, the tools at hand are a big part of the process for a lot of writers. You probably have your favorite word processing tool, or maybe you're a legal pad or even a typewriter user. Whatever works for you is best. If you're starting out and looking for ideas, the word-processing program I recommend for rough draft short pieces is TextEdit on a Mac. WordPad is the PC equivalent. Microsoft Word is best avoided; it's unnecessarily cumbersome. For longer work, like a novel, Scrivener is best.

PROTECTING YOUR WORK

Some people work in Google Drive, which automatically backs up while you work. It makes me nervous to have my work only saved on an external drive somewhere that I can't control. How do I know someone's not going to make a mistake and delete everything? I'm comforted to know my writing is somewhere on my hard drive or in my actual possession. If I ever use Google Drive to write (and sometimes I find myself giving notes to other people this way), I back it up to my own computer. But if you're comfortable with Google Drive or a similar online backup system, great.

It's obviously a good idea to back up your writing, which is another integral part of any writing process. One of the worst things that can happen to a writer is writing something brilliant and then losing it forever. It's heartbreaking.

If you don't have a good backup system, at least email your writing to yourself. Eventually, get an external drive and back up your work every day, or use a program like Time Machine to automatically back up as you write.

Beyond backups, when it comes to protecting their work, a lot of beginning writers worry their work might be stolen. People who don't write very much are often the ones most concerned about this, and it's possible they only dwell on the matter as a subconscious excuse to avoid writing. The simple solution to this worry is to ignore it. There are steps you can take to protect your work, but if you're just writing short comedy pieces, you don't have to worry about theft. If you want to submit a piece to a magazine or website and it would make you feel better to protect it, mail it to yourself and keep the letter sealed when you receive it. This is the cheapest way to prove you wrote the piece, which you will never have to do. An even more secure way to prove authorship is to send it to the Library of Congress and pay for an official copyright ($35). But this is overkill. Common Law copyright says as soon as you create something, you own the copyright. The only justification for officially copyrighting a piece of writing is when you publish it. If you write a screenplay, register it with the Writer's Guild. (Anyone can do this for $20. Students and WGA members get a discount.) If you write a book and send it out to agents and publishers, there's no need to copyright it. None of those people are going to steal your work—it would be a career-ending mistake for any of them, and it wouldn't be worth what little they might gain from it. If they think your work is amazing, they'd make so much more money by making a legitimate book deal with you and publishing your book. But if you self-publish your book on Amazon, copyright it.

Theft of writing almost never happens, but these simple actions can at least give you piece of mind. If anyone ever tries to steal your work, make sure you have evidence that it's yours, then send them a letter asking them to stop. To be clear, by "stealing," I mean repeating sentences you wrote verbatim—actual plagiarism. If someone merely uses your themes, concepts, book titles or screenplay titles, those things aren't protected by copyright. And if anyone ever creates anything similar to something you wrote in this way, either wittingly or unwittingly, you're best off being flattered that your idea was good enough to be thought up twice, ignore it, and move on.

FLOW STATE

If your calendar is freed up on a given day, feel free to extend the amount of time you write, or better yet, allow yourself to become immersed in your writing. When this happens, you may begin to forget what time it is. You may experience a sense that you've transcended time and space. This is "flow state," the holy grail of any writing process. When you enter flow state, you'll produce an untold abundance of writing, and you'll find it tremendously satisfying. You'll feel like you're merely a vessel through which some unseen force is producing voluminous work. Getting "in the zone" like this is the rush every creative person craves. Once you experience it, you may become addicted to it.

CHAPTER 12 ACTION STEPS

1. Establish a trigger, routine, and reward.

2. Write for a set amount of time using your trigger, routine, and reward for 30 days to make writing a daily habit.

13

THE PROBLEM
WITH SECOND DRAFTS

Most beginning writers approach second drafts as final drafts. They fix a couple of typos and maybe improve one joke. But the sad reality is that most first drafts don't work. They usually need to be completely rewritten.

The problem is, the writers afflicted with this problem don't realize it. They can't see it because they're too close to it. They're biased. Furthermore, their feedback group doesn't realize it either. And if they do, they rarely speak up about it. Instead, they're polite. They sugarcoat their feedback. The end result is a second draft that's barely better than the first, and a piece that's not going to excite readers.

Feedback, as flawed as it can be, is an essential step between your first and second drafts. You need to get out of your head and get a fresh perspective on your piece.

Despite all your efforts, it's rare that a first draft has the right take and the best joke beats. This is an important realization you need to have at this stage in the process. But it's only a problem if you fail to deal with it.

You may feel like you're working at crossed purposes, especially after completing a first draft that clearly doesn't work. Sometimes you have to take a step backwards in order to clearly see the right path forward.

Knowing how to interpret feedback, including how to read between the lines of any polite feedback, will help you tackle this problem and eliminate it.

Here's how most feedback works:

Your piece isn't working. It probably has the wrong take. Whatever the case, something glaring is wrong with it, but no one in your feedback group can see it. You certainly can't see it. To spare your feelings, your feedback group won't tell you your piece has the wrong take even if they could articulate the problem. Instead, they'll tell you about the one joke they saw in your piece that they thought was funny. Others will agree. And your piece probably does indeed have one funny joke in it.

This is some of the most counterproductive feedback you can get. You'll get excited that you wrote a funny line. You'll be so excited that you'll hold onto that line for dear life, refusing to cut it in subsequent drafts. You'll forget the rule of good writing, "kill your darlings." That line is probably dragging your whole piece down and you don't realize it. That line is probably off-take. It gets a laugh at the expense of your overall concept, not in service of it. It's like a bomb that goes off in your piece, making it nearly impossible to put the pieces back together.

What you need is someone who can give you the feedback, "Your piece isn't working. It's off-take. This one joke is funny, but it's unrelated to your core joke. You should cut that joke and rewrite this." But it will probably be a long time before you find someone who can talk so straight.

After you find peers in writers groups, or new friends from an improv class, you may get close to getting the kind of critical feedback you need, but politeness will always be at play in social groups, and that politeness will usually crush any meaningful constructive feedback. In-person feedback from non-professionals will rarely be as objective and honest as online feedback. People who know you in real life will go a lot further than an online acquaintance to protect your feelings from harsh though necessary opinion. They'll soften their critique and point out your one good joke but avoid telling you your whole piece isn't working. This all-too-common scenario must be avoided.

Feedback groups for prose are called "beta readers." They're beta-testing your work to report any bugs. You'll fix these bugs in your second draft. Use the same guidelines for finding beta readers as you did for finding feedback groups on your ideas. To start, use the same people as both your feedback group and your beta readers. Those who remember your initial title idea when they first reviewed your jokes will have a valuable perspective, and their expectations for your piece will give you good information. But it's also wise to include some new people in your group of beta readers, people who have never heard your title idea before. These types of beta readers can give you insight into the mind of the uninitiated reader, or at least a close approximation of the uninitiated reader.

Ask your beta readers to read your piece as if they simply stumbled upon it at random and don't know you. If you know them personally, they'll still be biased, but providing this context will at least put them in the best frame of mind, encourage them to keep their bias in check, and incentivize them to be as honest as possible under the circumstances.

There are eight ways to get the most out of any feedback you receive on a piece of prose:

1. Ask specific questions. Asking your beta readers for general notes can be helpful, but you can maximize the quality of your feedback by asking for specifics you can actually use. Try these questions:

- Did you think the title was funny? Did it work? If not, why not? What would make it work?
- Did the piece grab you and make you laugh in the first line or two? If not, what would it need to do to grab you?
- Did the piece pull you in more as you read, or did you feel like you wanted to

stop reading at any point? If so, where was that?

- Did the piece get funnier and funnier as it went along, or were there lulls in the laugh-meter? If so, where were those lulls?
- Did you like the way the piece ended? Could it have ended funnier?
- Did the piece seem to stick to the subject at hand, or did it seem to veer off course anywhere? If so, where?
- What suggestions do you have for improving the piece?
- Overall, did the piece hold your attention? Did you like it?

Ask them to rate your piece using a star rating system, 1 star being awful and 10 stars being the funniest thing they've ever read.

2. Take as many notes as possible from your beta readers.

Ask for written notes. If they're unable to do this, or you meet with them in person or talk on the phone, get their permission to record them. Everything your beta readers say about your piece is valuable intel, and you want to have a clear record of it all that you can reference later.

3. Listen to the "no's."

Maybe your piece is great, and that's wonderful news that you should feel good about, but chances are, if your beta reader says your piece is great, they're simply being lazy or too nice. Any piece can be improved. When your beta readers like a piece and see no room for improvement, be skeptical.

On the other hand, when your beta readers don't like a piece, you can confidently rely on that information, especially if more than one beta reader says they don't like it. Beta readers as a whole are almost always far kinder than a real audience will be. However many stars your beta readers rate your piece, real readers out in the real world will rate it at least 2 to 3 stars lower. Real readers will always be harsher because they're not invested. They don't care about you. The fact that your beta readers care enough to give you feedback makes them biased. Beta readers will almost always find something positive to say about your piece. But a reader won't. However, if you get lucky and your beta readers don't like your piece and also let you know this fact, then you know your piece is truly in need of a major retooling.

If they don't like a specific joke—especially if several different beta readers point out the same joke for being weak, telling you it wasn't working or was confusing, believe them. They're right. "No's" like this will likely be under-represented, so you need to give extra weight to them when they emerge.

FUNNIER-WRITING TIP #16: CREATE A LACK OF AWARENESS

Most comedy stories involve one or more layers of unawareness. It may be characters in the piece who don't recognize that their world is askew. It may be that the editorial voice is unaware of its obvious bias or misplaced focus. It may be characters in the piece not realizing they live in a skewed, comic world. It may be the writer of the piece (the voice behind the curtain—yours) pretending not to be aware the piece is supposed to be funny. Sometimes when pieces aren't as funny as they could be, or aren't playing it as straight as they could be, a lack of awareness on some level is the element that's missing. Look at your piece and see if there's a clear lack of awareness among your characters or your own voice.

Only believe a story is great if *all* your beta readers say it's great. If some say it's great and some say it's not working, believe the latter. They're the most accurate. At the very least, their notes can provide you with clues as to how to improve your piece, no matter how great it may be.

If more than one beta reader points out the same part of your piece and tells you it's weak, this is an obvious clue that there's something wrong with that part. Your beta readers may not know exactly what the problem is or what the solution is, but when they all point to the same area, they nonetheless give you great insight into where your piece needs work. It could be that you veer off-take at that point and perhaps never regained your footing. It could be that you simply have a weak joke beat there. Once you have the feedback, you can diagnose the problem and fix it by staying on-take or brainstorming better joke beats.

a good second draft

4. Consider every negative comment a gift.

When someone makes a negative comment about the comedy piece you worked hard on, it can feel like a punch to the gut. This is most writers' initial reaction. But you need to reframe this experience as a positive one. A negative comment is a gift, a rare peek inside a real reader's mind, and you need to welcome it. Cherish it, learn from it, and know that you can use this valuable information to improve your writing. Without it, you might have never known what was wrong with your piece.

Negative comments are the secret sauce that will make your piece great. Without them, you're flying blind, awash in the polite and positive feedback you'll get from most beta readers. They're trying to be supportive, and they're well intentioned, but they're often not giving you the constructive, roll-up-your-sleeves feedback you need.

5. Be skeptical of your own writing.

Look at your writing not as gospel, but as something malleable, always improvable. If your beta readers aren't pointing out a certain joke beat in your piece and saying it's hilarious, don't just keep such mediocre beats in your second draft; rewrite them until people point them out as particularly hilarious. The feedback you ultimately want to get on your piece is, "I thought it was hilarious from start to finish and only got funnier as it went along!" Beta readers may not be so articulate with their feedback, but if they thought all the joke beats worked, they'll say things like, "The whole piece was great," "It was super funny throughout," "There wasn't a dull moment," or they'll have trouble telling you how great the piece was because they're laughing too hard. That's when you know you've cracked the code and written a good piece.

It will probably take you more than a second draft to get to this level of quality. It may not even be possible to get there with your current story. You may need to pick another title and write a few more pieces to get there. But if you always remain skeptical of how good your writing is, and are careful to give credence to your beta readers' negative reactions, you'll have the right mindset to continue improving your writing until it works the best it can to generate laughs.

6. Don't fall in love.

If you have a soft spot for any joke beat in your piece, you must be open to changing it if enough of your beta readers tell you it's not working. If no one mentions a particular beat, know that it's just average and therefore not helping you. Let your beta readers tell you what's working and trust their judgment over your own.

If you fall in love with a phrase or joke beat, you'll lose objectivity and won't be able to make the choice to cut that section if in fact it needs to be cut.

On rare occasion, all your beta readers will tell you the joke beat you love is terrible, but they'll be wrong because you have some secret knowledge as to why the joke beat is golden. But for now, trust your beta readers. In time, this will build up your own internal barometer for what works and what doesn't. If you fall in love with too much of your work, ignore your readers, and rely too much on your own sense of humor, you'll never develop a good, reliable inner Editor.

7. Don't be afraid to ask for more jokes.

If you get lukewarm feedback from your beta readers and feel stymied, or if you feel like you've come up with all the joke beats you possibly can for your piece but they're still not wowing your beta readers, ask them for suggestions of other joke beats you could add. Your beta readers might have been helping you come up with joke beats before you wrote your piece, but now is different. Now they have a draft in front of them, so their suggestions will be more on-take. People have a remarkable ability to see the potential of a piece after it's written out in front of them. Before a piece is written, they often have a hard time envisioning it the same way the writer does, and will be hit-or-miss with their joke-beat suggestions. Once they see it, their suggestions could give your piece just the boost it needs.

If you can get every one of your beta readers to give you 2–3 additional joke beat ideas, you'll likely have a wealth of possibilities for punching up your piece. Some of these suggestions won't be good, of course, but if you're only writing a half page or so, a few more joke-beat suggestions that are funnier than the ones you currently have could make a big difference.

Some of the new joke beats your beta readers suggest might be so good that they help you see even greater humor potential in your piece, spurring you to come up with better joke beats or even a better take than you were working with previously. A few joke suggestions at this stage have the potential to give your piece a major upgrade.

You may be wondering if you deserve to take credit for writing a piece when someone else brainstormed key jokes for you. It's a good thing to figure out before you publish. If you're the one putting all the words down and you came up with the title and you got someone's permission to use their suggested joke beat, you're well within your rights to take all the credit. It's rare that a work of writing is done in solitude. Writers often work with beta readers, copyeditors, and editors who help them rephrase ideas and reshape sentences. If you want to credit someone who helped you significantly, that's up to you, but the standard practice in the industry is that all writers help each other punch up their work, and no one expects credit for a couple of joke suggestions. Besides, you'll do the same for them, and you won't demand credit for any of your jokes either. You offer them up in the spirit of helping someone write a good piece.

8. Make sure you have the confidence to proceed.

Stop asking your beta readers for more jokes or more feedback notes only when you've received enough notes to give you a clear idea how your piece needs to be reworked. When you're confident you have new, better joke beats or a refined take, you're ready to go to the next step.

If you feel like you've gotten enough good information and feel confident you know how to rewrite your piece, do it now, while the feedback is fresh in your mind. Refer to your beta readers' notes or recordings as you write.

If you find you're still unsure how to proceed after getting notes from beta readers, bang out a second draft anyway, learn what you can, and then write another piece, one that appeals to you more. Writing more pieces will build your confidence, and each one will get progressively easier to write.

After you write this second draft, let it sit for a while, just like you did your first draft. You may not have to let it sit quite as long. Maybe just a day, long enough to let your mind focus on something else for a while. Pass it off to your beta readers again to get their reaction. Include a couple of new people who've never seen your title or any draft.

If you get notes, do a third draft. If you're still tinkering after a third or fourth draft, finish it as best you can and move on to another idea. It's important you don't spin your wheels on this process, especially if this is one of the first pieces you've written. This is a quagmire that can easily sink a writer's future.

When you have a draft that your beta readers like, read it quickly and disinterestedly, as a reader would, just to make sure it's as accessible as you can make it. Then read it carefully, correct any typos, and spell-check it. This is your final draft. And it's ready to send out to the world.

I recommend you post your story online. Find a picture for it and put in on Instagram, upload it to Medium, put it on your blog—wherever you like. Put your piece out there, even if it feels scary. Just ignore the fear and do it. This is how all writers get started.

Most importantly, write another piece. Go through the process again. This is what writers do.

What does a second draft look like? Here's the second draft of Robert's cardboard-box piece:

Man Flattening Cardboard Box Tastes True Power

Brad Saunders never sought power. By all accounts, the unassuming logistics consultant and father of two was content to toil in a habitual station of abject obedience. But all that changed the moment he took hold of a 20-by-24-inch corrugated cardboard shipping box and collapsed it, sending shockwaves throughout his block and tasting true power for the first time in his otherwise unassuming existence.

The man bellowed guttural, almost beastly roars that could be heard as far as 20 feet away from the trash bins aside his garage where he stood. It was the world's first glimpse into the volcanic, megalomaniac fissure that opened in Saunders as he expressed the unstoppable desire to bend and reshape the box to meet his unrelenting will.

"Not this time," he stated with an arrogant snort as he thrust the box into the recycling bin.

Clare Mercer, who observed Saunders' raw demonstration of brute force while walking her dog, described the manner in which her neighbor punched the box, severing tape from flap with bare sinew, remaking the container in his own twisted design. But even after the box was compressed and flattened, this suburban übermensch was not finished.

"There was a fearsome crack as he took the box and just hammered it," Mercer said, a tremble of awe in her voice. "Honestly, it frightened me a little, but I also found it magnetic. It made me want to follow him into battle, to storm the gates of hell."

Having decimated the box, the rogue demigod slammed the recycling-bin lid closed with a newfound and commanding strength. He then shuffled back home and reportedly asked his wife what else she needed him to do.

Note how he changed the format slightly, going from a hard-news parody format to more of a magazine feature piece. Most of his joke beats were changed and improved. The piece also has more verisimilitude, heightened contrast, is played more straight, and has nicely escalating joke beats that each get at the heart of the joke promised in the title. He also made the piece easier to read with frequent paragraph breaks. This always makes a piece of prose more welcoming to a reader.

Robert sold the piece to *Blaffo*. It was accompanied by a faux-live smartphone video of the man crushing the box.

CHAPTER 13 ACTION STEPS

1. Give your first draft to a team of beta readers and ask for specific notes on how you can improve it.

2. Write a second draft based on the notes you get from your beta readers.

3. Show your second draft to beta readers for a second round of notes.

4. When your beta readers like what you've done, give your piece a polish.

5. Send this final draft out into the world.

14

MORE EXAMPLES

You've seen the example of Robert's cardboard-box piece as we've gone through the process of writing a comedy piece. In this chapter, you'll see other real-world examples of short comedy from various writers, most of them students of mine. Each example will start, if possible, at the idea stage and go all the way to publication, if the piece was published.

By looking at these examples, which come in different formats and different media, you'll get a good look at the path all short comedy pieces take. It's laid it out for you in the previous chapters, but this time it'll be unencumbered by theory, tips, or best practices; this time it's from the writer's perspective, and you'll see the actual results.

In some cases the pieces didn't work or didn't go through the entire process, and in many cases you'll see that not necessarily all the steps were followed. This is what happens. Things don't always get done perfectly or according to an ideal plan. You'll get the best results following every step of the process, especially if you're a beginner, but for now here's an accurate and sometimes flawed depiction of typical ways the process plays out.

Both comedy and feedback are presented in their original form, without editing or corrections.

EXAMPLE 1: OFFICE FIRE

Writer Ben Thompson started with a list of 10 jokes:

1. *Human-caused climate change ranked world's #1 natural disaster*
2. *Pruitt blames floundering Gulf Coast on angry cod.*
3. *Neighbors fear for homeless baby after cradle robbing.*
4. *Woman dumps sugar daddy after he turns sour.*
5. *Local man in park caught beating around the bush.*
6. *Asshole friend tired of being the butt of all jokes.*
7. *Opioids: Learn all the juicy facts behind America's hottest trend*
8. *Today's forecast: Rainy with a chance of nuclear fallout*
9. *"And this year's Academy Award for best Feature Documentary goes to Tyler Perry, for Madea 20: Madea's Diary of a Diabetic."*
10. *Missed Connection: We locked eyes during office building fire - m4w – 30*

The last joke on his list jumped out to his feedback group because it's funny and original: a parody of a "missed connection" personal ad. This isn't something that's been done a lot in prose comedy, so it feels fresh. It also has great contrast: the frivolousness of a missed connection compared to the panic of an office fire. It's one of those great, simple title ideas that immediately unfolds as soon as you see it—you can start to imagine how the piece would build.

The medium, format, structure, and take were obvious to Ben: it's a parody of a personal ad, so the medium would be prose, the format would be a personal-ad parody, and the take should escalate the Irony (heightening the contrast) of a tragic fire as compared to the light, playful tone of a personal ad.

The riffs Ben got from his feedback group gave him a few of the joke beats he used in his first draft:

Missed Connection: We locked eyes during office building fire - M4W - 30

This might be a bit of a long shot but I was across the room from you on the 4th floor of the Gunnar/Fraska office when the building went up in flames last week. I remember as smoke billowed into the room you looked like an angel descending through the clouds from heaven. Then the fire began to grow, lighting up your caramel colored hair, and as the rising flames danced I became entranced, wondering if someday we too might dance in the heat of passion. It wasn't long after that the smoke forced us to the ground, and it was there for a split second our eyes met. I tried calling out to ask for your number, but a fireman carried you away. You looked back at me through the raging inferno and I thought, could this be a metaphor for the fire building in my heart?

I think we made a deep connection that day. If you see this ad...please write back and tell me which one of my limbs was caught under the fallen rafter. I hope you don't mind third degree burns...would love to grab coffee someday....perhaps after my next skin graft.

Ben wrote an uncommonly good first draft. Blessed with a simple and funny title, he rose to the challenge by staying on track and spooling out joke beats.

From the title you might expect this piece to be more formulaic than satirical. But Subtext not evident at the title stage reveals itself in the draft. The piece says people try to find love despite the fact that we're doomed to a life of tragedy. It's a "flaw" in humanity that's not much of a flaw at all. It's a romantic, uplifting and life-affirming trait. Satire doesn't always have to be negative; it can point out any human frailty, positive or negative. Ben keeps the strong value judgement subtextual and focuses on the joke beats, making the piece widely accessible.

The piece uses a few Funny Filters. Irony and Parody are the primary forces at work in the title, and accordingly the primary drivers of the piece. But there's also Misplaced Focus, with the man focusing on a trivial thing (locking eyes with a woman) while ignoring the elephant in the room (the office fire). There's Character as well, with this man as the Everyman archetype, acting on his trait (acting normal). In comedy, the Everyman archetype is typically thrust into extraordinary circumstances to create contrast.

There's great verisimilitude here as well. The piece sounds exactly like a real missed-connection personal ad. Ben mimics the conversational style of such ads and never breaks voice. The reader imagines this character as nonsensical and comedic, yet senses the intelligent writer behind the curtain, creating a funny lack of awareness on two levels: the writer pretending to be unaware the piece is funny, and the character of the man unaware that he's focusing on something trivial in the face of a life-and-death emergency.

Another good thing about this draft is the first joke beat ("when the building went up in flames last week"), which doesn't merely repeat the joke of the title; it escalates it slightly by filling out a few small details of the comedy world, using different wording to describe the fire, and heighten the contrast with a casual tone. The first joke beat of too many short comedy pieces merely repeats the joke beat of the title. It's best to escalate the second joke beat so the audience knows they're in for a fun ride.

The feedback Ben got on this story was that he could have escalated the absurdity more. He could have made the woman more clearly injured, possibly even burned to death at the end, making the man even more unaware, flippant with, "Did we miss our chance for romance as you were engulfed by flames instead of by my passion?" or, "Still alive? Maybe we'll have another chance encounter in the burn unit."

Here's his second draft:

MISSED CONNECTION: WE LOCKED EYES DURING OFFICE BUILDING FIRE - M4W - 30

This might be a bit of a long shot but I was across the room from you on the 4th floor of the Gunnar/Fraska office when the building went up in flames last week. I remember as smoke billowed into the room you looked like an angel descending through the clouds from heaven. Then fire swept through, literally lighting up your caramel colored hair. The caramel changed to a beautiful red in an instant, but to me it felt like a lifetime. As the blaze spread to your body I became entranced watching you dance in tune with each flicker of flame. I know you were trying to shake off the fire, but I stood there wondering if maybe someday you and I might find ourselves consumed in a passionate dance. Not long after the smoke forced me to the ground, and you elegantly executed the stop-drop-and-roll. And it was there on the floor where our eyes met for a split second. I tried to ask for your number, but a fireman carried you away your beautiful mutilated body before I could shout out to you. You just looked back at me through the raging inferno; your melting face melting my heart.

Did we make a connection there in that room? Or did dousing the fire extinguish our chance for romance? Because I can't help but wish it had been my love that engulfed you that day. If you're still alive and see this, please write back and tell me which one of my limbs was caught under the fallen rafter. I'd love to take you out. If it's not too soon, perhaps we could stoke the spark of romance with a hot couples massage? Until then I'll be waiting for a chance encounter with you in the burn unit.

Ben's second draft wasn't rewritten much, since the first draft was in good shape. But he heightened the contrast and lack of awareness further. Other changes were lateral. It's still a good piece with solid joke beats.

The feedback he got on his second draft was to tighten it so it's shorter, more like the length of a typical personal ad.

His final draft:

Missed Connection: We locked eyes during office building fire - M4W - 30

This might be a bit of a long shot but I was across the room from you on the 4th floor of the Gunnar/Fraska building when it went up in flames. I remember as smoke billowed into the room you looked like an angel descending through the clouds from heaven. The fire quickly swept through, literally lighting up your caramel colored hair. It happened in an instant, but to me it felt like a lifetime. When the blaze spread to your body I became entranced watching you rhythmically move in tune with each flickering flame, and I stood there wondering if maybe someday we might find ourselves consumed in our own passionate dance. It was after the smoke forced me to the ground that our eyes met for a split second. I wanted to ask for your number, but a fireman carried away your beautiful mutilated body before I could shout out to you. You just looked back through the raging inferno; your melting face melting my heart.

Did we make a connection there in that room? Because I can't help but wish it had been my love that engulfed you that day. If you're still alive and see this I'd love to take you out. Perhaps we could stoke the spark of romance with a fondue dinner? Until then I'll be waiting for a chance encounter with you in the burn unit.

The joke beats are tight and escalate well. Ben reigned in the long second draft to make for a nice little piece.

He submitted it to *McSweeney's* but was rejected. Nonetheless, this is an excellent piece to post on a blog or use as part of a writing portfolio or submission packet. It demonstrates competence staying on-take with joke beats and escalating them along a simple and clear track.

If he wanted to be enterprising, Ben could run this as a real personal ad, turning it into street art.

EXAMPLE 2: UNEMPLOYED ACTRESS

Christina Devlin also started with a list of ten ideas:

1. *"Will One of You Kids Please Answer Me?" Asks Dora the Explorer*
2. *North Korean Olympic Hopefuls Found Medaling in South Korean Athletic Affairs*
3. *Yoga Instructor's Murder Confession Shrouded in Soothing Tones During Final Meditation*
4. *Bucket's List Includes Things to Do Before Kicking Itself*
5. *Unemployed Actress Accepts Venti Vanilla Latte, Thanks Everyone at the Starbucks on Sunset for Making It Possible*

6. *Cupid's OKCUPID Profile Kind of Sketchy*

7. *Clear Skies Ahead for Weather Man's Stormy Relationship with Weather Girl*

8. *TED Talks and You're Not Going to Like What He Has to Say*

9. *Guitar Player Strung Out on Band's Musical Discord*

10. *Death by Chocolate Recipe Sure to Stop the Heart of Any Beau This Valentine's Day*

She chose number five on her list because it has legs—she could start to see it unfolding. The format is clear from the title: this is a parody of an award acceptance speech. The structure is also evident in the title: this is an Analogy between accepting a latte (overt) and accepting a prestigious entertainment-industry award (hidden), so Analogy structure should be used to map acceptance-speech tropes onto a typical Starbucks purchase.

Here's her first draft:

UNEMPLOYED ACTRESS ACCEPTS VENTI VANILLA LATTE, THANKS EVERYONE AT THE STARBUCKS ON SUNSET FOR MAKING IT POSSIBLE

First and foremost, I'd like to thank this Starbucks on Sunset for making this delicious Venti Vanilla Latte, on this busy Monday morning, here in Los Angeles. To all the other coffees I could have chosen in the "specialty drink" category—Carmel Macchiato, Flat White, Mocha Frappuccino and Cappuccino—as well as the other coffee shops on Sunset – Javista Organic Coffee Bar, Blackwood Coffee Bar, The Coffee Bean and Tea Leaf and Coffee Commissary—you are all so extraordinary and I admire you more than I can put into words spelled out in coffee beans, so thank you for just being available as a choice.

It's been the greatest honor just to stand in line, here at Starbucks on Sunset, watching each and every barista work quickly and happily to fulfill my drink order. To Corey Smelt, Manager of Starbucks on Sunset, I have come to depend on you to make sure this location is stocked with Venti cups, Vanilla syrup and espresso beans and I cannot thank you enough for being well-prepared and receptive to my suggestions and demands.

To Debbie, Matt and the redheaded barista, who always comments on my highlights, I thank you for crafting this latte to my satisfaction and taking the extra time to include a fancy little heart in its frothy milk.

To my fellow customers of Starbucks on Sunset, I thank you for waiting patiently as I took my time ordering my drink, toggling back and forth between syrups and sizes and asking questions about dairy options and fair-trade agreements within the coffee industry. I am aware this can be annoying and even make you late for work, so, again, I thank you for believing in me.

Last, but not least, I want to thank my parents for continuing to send me money, at age 30, so I can afford to drink this Venti Vanilla Latte and take it back to the apartment, for which they pay, to binge-watch Netflix and wait for a callback from any of the directors, for which I auditioned this week, and this year. And to my caffeine addiction, which stood by me all these years, and brought me here to Starbucks on Sunset when this aspiring actress from Idaho was looking for a quick fix, couldn't find her way around Hollywood and was too scared to trust anything other than big name franchises, I am in your debt.

I do realize that this has all been a huge confluence of luck and opportunity. I'm so grateful to have been handed this warm beverage without judgment and with a smile this morning, since I did not get the part of Waitress 2 in the new Greta Gerwig movie and am seriously thinking of moving back to Idaho and asking for my job back at JC Penney.

To the entire crew, here at Starbucks on Sunset, who put their heart and soul into this Venti Vanilla Latte, I promise to come back every morning this week, like I did last week, and do this all over again because, well, I love this specialty drink and I love all of you for making it.

Thank you. Thank you. Thank you.

The feedback Christina got, which came from only one person, was that it was fantastic:

> "As far as your story goes, I really like it. I think it was a smart choice to write this in a first person perspective. I think you did a great job with analogy mapping. I love that you were able to find things about Starbucks to fill the typical beats of an award show speech. And the parody voice here is spot on. Honestly, I don't really have any notes. I like the stuff about her waiting for a call back, and I wonder if you could start hinting at her struggles as an actress a bit earlier in the piece. But overall, I thought this thing was very strong. Nice work."

I agree the piece is in excellent shape, and this feedback points out an important way to improve it: it needs to escalate sooner. The beats about her being a desperate actress struggling to make it in LA add to the contrast and therefore make this funnier. But they happen too late. We don't get to see the Irony of the hardscrabble pathos with the imagined glamour of an awards show up top, which would hook the reader. This was part of the promise of the headline, and if readers saw that this promise wasn't delivered quickly, they'd probably abandon the piece.

This feedback is an example of the positive yet flawed feedback a piece will often get. It's supportive, but misses an important shortcoming of the piece. The beta reader failed to mention the title, whereas for the reader the title is everything. This often happens with beta readers because they're too close to the piece and aren't experiencing it in the same context as the reader.

The problem with the title is that it doesn't match the story. This happens a lot, and it's an easy fix in this case. Often a title starts out in one format (in this instance, a fake-news headline), but then a new, more appropriate format is chosen for the piece during the format-selection stage (in this case a first-person monologue). When that happens, the title must also change to match the format. Readers will be confused if they think a piece is going to be one format but turns out to be another. It's jarring, and gives them another reason not to trust the writer.

So, for this piece, the headline needs to be changed to first-person: "As an Unemployed Actress, I Accept This Venti Vanilla Latte and Thank Everyone at the Starbucks on Sunset for Making It Possible."

Christina changed the title and submitted her piece to *McSweeney's*, but as of this writing hasn't heard back.

EXAMPLE 3: DISORIENTED MOUSE

Wes Marfield started with these ten ideas:

1. *Trump's Doctor Defends Controversial Work Taking Place In His Lab*
2. *Virgins Make Pact To Hack Accounts Of Popular Girls Before Prom*
3. *Moon Still Frequents Buzz Aldrin's Facebook Page*
4. *Line Forms Outside Beyoncé Concert As Fans Are Let In Two-By-Two*
5. *Russian Schoolchildren Awed When CIA Drone Emerges From Caterpil-*

     lar's Cocoon

6. *New Police Body Camera Includes Built-In Narration From James Woods*

7. *Disoriented Mouse Shot To Protect Child Who Wandered Into Chuck E. Cheese Habitat*

8. *Driverless Car Not Sure Where That Weed Came From*

9. *Man Prays For Peaceful Resolution As Erection Situation Heads Into Its Fifth Hour*

10. *Wedding DJ Hopes His Big Day Goes Off Without A Hitch*

He chose number eight, and decided to write it as a news-parody story, since the title sounded like a news headline:

Driverless Car Not Sure Where That Weed Came From

PALO ALTO—After being pulled over for driving the wrong way on a divided highway, a driverless Volkswagen Passat couldn't explain the marijuana found in the automobile's glove box. "I'm, uh, just driving my buddy's car for the night," a voice emanating from somewhere in the front seat told officers on the scene, who found the drugs after suspicion of the driver's inebriation led to a search of the vehicle. "The telltale signs were all there," California Highway Patrol officer Pete Franklin said. "The erratic driving, the pot smell, the dilated apertures–it was clear whoever was remotely piloting this vehicle had been smoking marijuana. So we read the automobile its rights and placed it under arrest." But as Franklin waited on backup to haul the Volkswagen off to impound, the vehicle magically restarted itself and fled the scene. It was last spotted blowing through the intersection in front of a Del Taco.

The feedback he got, which happened to be from me, was that the headline was confusing:

> "Oh, *that* kind of weed! I was thinking it was a weed in the road, or growing on the side of the road, like weeds do. I'm not sure what the Funny Filter at work is here, besides a little Shock. Mistaken identity is not a Funny Filter. As the story goes on, you do a good job of extracting an Analogy between a human driver and a self-driving car, but it's too little too late. Also, if this is to be a news-story Parody, you can't bury the lede like that. If a drunk driver fled the scene of an arrest and was at large, that would be the headline."

Wes struggled with the piece, wondering if he picked the wrong headline. This is something that happens often to writers, creates a lot of extra work, and is a consequence of not getting enough good feedback on the initial ideas. Number eight doesn't have legs and isn't exactly understandable from the title alone. It shouldn't have passed muster during the title-selection process.

He liked number seven too, so he decided to write that one instead. He found it much easier:

Disoriented Mouse Shot To Protect Child Who Wandered Into Chuck E. Cheese Habitat

TUSCON—Chuck E. Cheese employees shot and killed a giant animatronic rat on Saturday after a six-year-old boy attempted to give it a hug, onlookers reported. Chuck, a 19-year old, 700 pound member of the endangered croonerus rodentia family, was gunned down mid-performance when the boy darted over to the stage from the ball pit before anyone had a chance to stop him. "The child did not appear to be under attack," store manager Brandon Phipps said, "But any time a human is within arm's reach of a volatile animal like that, it's considered a life-threatening situation. We had no choice but to take him down." The child, whose name isn't being released, was taken to an area hospital to be treated with Adderall for non-life threatening injuries. Several horrified onlookers were upset at the drastic measures taken by the family-friendly pizza restaurant. "It was disturbing," local mother of two Sharon Waters said, "He didn't die right away. After they shot him he just stood there stammering 'Everything Is Awesome' for a few seconds in a pool of his own sparks." Phipps said his team considered the use of non-lethal force, but decided against it in the best interest of the child. "Chuck E. Cheese-issued tranc darts aren't effective if the violator doesn't have a bloodstream, and unplugging it wouldn't have worked since these particular models can hold a charge for a good two hours," Phipps said. The restaurant will be closed indefinitely pending a full investigation by the local authorities and PETA.

Wes came up with a solid Analogy structure, comparing an animatronic mouse at Chuck E. Cheese to a wild animal at the zoo. It's a good take. Here's the feedback I gave him:

"Great job on this! There are a few places up top where you could tweak it to sound more like a zoo incident, such as losing 'disoriented' from the headline—that word is not helping you. Also, changing the lede:

"A six-year-old is in unharmed after accidentally falling into an enclosed jamboree chamber at the Lincoln Ave Chuck E. Cheese Thursday. Restaurant officials armed with tranc guns were called to the scene and made the decision to kill the animal, a full-grown, freakishly large banjo-playing mouse. Onlookers gasped as they watched a beast four times the boy's size move quickly toward the child with a menacing, dancing-type motion. It then appeared to grab the boy. 'We weren't sure at first if he was hugging him or trying to protect him from the other very large animals in the enclosure,' one witness said. The other animals were identifed by witnesses as a bear wearing a straw hat, a very happy moose, and 'other rodents.'

"- okay, I'm getting carried away, but that's the type of thing I'm talking about. Really channel those zoo stories. The connections between the two parts of the analogy are where the jokes are. Later in the piece you make more connections, so you have a lot on the whole. I just thought it was slow to get started, and you really want to establish the joke and the structure right away."

The Chuck E. Cheese piece wasn't published anywhere, but Wes kept trying. Eventually he got work published in *The New Yorker*'s "Shouts & Murmurs" column and elsewhere.

He told me the last two pieces he sold also began with weak premises that he scrapped in favor of new titles. Sometimes you have to start writing a piece to realize the concept doesn't work, which allows you to see more clearly what will.

EXAMPLE 4:
'LOST DOG' POSTERS

Ricardo Angulo started with a list of ten project ideas:

> 1. *MyDelaware.Gov (Fake website for the state of Delaware; implies Delaware is weird fantastical Twin Peaks land.)*
> 2. *Duck, Duck, Goof! Jokebook For Yucksters LOL! (Fake Jokebook, Not Funny.)*

3. *Happy New Year Resolution! My Journey... (Blog by lazy character who tries to learn a hobby and lose weight by end of the year. Does neither.)*

4. *Missing Pet Posters (Fake missing posters from a bad, dumb pet owner. All the pets go missing in madcappy, hyperbolic way; implies they tried to escape him.)*

5. *InZinity (Fake contemporary zine prepared by a character who's generally an unpleasant try-hard.)*

6. *Comprehensive Guide To Rule Middle Management (career advice for commonplace work experiences, like getting an internship, improving your resume, but Machiavellian to an extreme.)*

7. *An Oral History Of My Dumb Fucking Lame-Ass Fucking Stepdad (An oral history of a teenager's stepfather, all his sources are biased, probably just his friends talking shit about his stepfather)*

8. *Bachelor's Cookbook (Fake cookbook that progressively shows the character is in some sort of deep depression.)*

9. *Principolitan (Cosmopolitan parody but with a severely Machiavellian bent.)*

10. *Coloring Outside The Lines! (Coloring book, but with no lines)*

WANTED

DEAD OR ALIVE

"PRINCESS TUTU"

Female, 1 year-old, 4.8 lbs, White W/ Black Patches,  Microchipped
Wanted for Robbery of the NEIGHBORS STRAWBERRY BUSH
and the PEMBROOK BATHROOM SLIPPERS

REWARD

☞ $$$200$$$ ☜

$50 Each Paw

for CAPTURE and PUNISHMENT of the Maltese, and return of the
Silver Bone-Shaped Dog Tag

Poster One

Number four jumped out at Ricardo and his feedback group. The idea
was, he would create fake missing pet posters and post them around town,
creating some edgy original street art.

The take he hatched was that the posters would suggest the dogs had
escaped their owners, but after riffing on it with his feedback group, he
settled on a different angle. (See Poster One, above.) Such radical take

FOUND , LOST

Then Found Again, Then Lost

Last seen on the intersection of Montrose & Ashland on December 1st, 8AM, but first found on Broadway & Halsted on November 26th at 4PM, then lost on the corner of Touhy & Wolcott on November 28th but found again on November 30th in Evanston.

Still Lost, If Found

Contact: 1-(800) 400-████

Or number of first owner if found

Poster Two

departures often happen in first drafts, when the writer either forgets the First Laugh (Funnier-Writing Tip #3, page 35), or finds in drafting that the original riffed take just doesn't hold up.

Upon review, Ricardo's feedback group decided the first draft of the poster was off-take, trying to do two things at once: parody both an Old West wanted poster and a lost-dog flyer. It was too complicated. It even included a joke beat that was off both takes: "Microchipped." It's not clear

Lost At Sea

REWARD!

<u>Identifying Features</u>: Female, 1 year-old, about 4.8 lbs., White Fur With Black Patches, Microchipped, Green Dog Collar, Very Shy, Approach With Caution As She Gets Scared Easy

<u>Last Seen</u>: Voyaging the high seas in the deadliest storm this side of Davy Jones locker. Ayy, the sea was angry that day, with a fog so murky you couldn't tell sky from sea. And the wind! Howling with rage as tremendous waves of the saltiest, coldest water rushed you left and right until you were submerged in the blackest of brine.

If Found, Contact: 1-(800)-400-▓▓▓▓

Poster Three

what take that joke serves. So, there was too much going on without a clear joke track. His feedback group recommended he focus on parodying only a "lost pet" poster.

For Ricardo's next draft, he produced a series of posters, each with a different take. (See Posters Two through Five, pages 144–147.)

Ricardo's second-draft posters work better. They each have a clear take, and all the joke beats within each poster align with each separate take (ex-

MISSING

KICKBALL

WHITE

SCUFFED

WITH BOOT PRINT

SLIGHTLY DEFLATED

LAST SEEN OVER THE FENCE

Contact: 1-(800)-400-████

Poster Four

cept for the unfortunate reappearance of "microchipped"). Ricardo got good feedback, especially on the edgiest poster ("Missing Kickball" on the following page), so he did a final design, coming up with more posters along the edgier line to fill out the series. (See Posters Six through Nine, pages 148–151.)

The last poster's hand-written text upped the verisimilitude even more. You might think these posters afflict the afflicted by making light of

FOR HIRE

Name: Princess Tutu

Breed: Maltese

Objective: To achieve growth and success in the real world

Experience:

House (02/2016-12/2016)   *Pet*
- Managed affairs of dog bed and throw pillows
- Fostered communication with local dogs at all hours

Freelancer (12/2016-Present)   *Lost*
- Maintained brand in the community
- Serve as outside liaison to squirrels

Skills & Expertise: Communication, Chew Toys (soft or otherwise), Digging, Streamlining Transference Of Dirt From Fur To Couch Cushions, Spanish Mastiff, Networking

Call (800)-524-▮▮▮▮ to hire expert ready to hit the ground running.

or Princess Tutu @ 800) 524 ▮ | or Princess Tutu @ 800) 524 ▮ | or Princess Tutu @ 800) 524 ▮ | or Princess Tutu @ 800) 524 ▮ | or Princess Tutu @ 800) 524 ▮ | or Princess Tutu @ 800) 524 ▮ | or Princess Tutu @ 800) 524 ▮ | or Princess Tutu @ 800) 524 ▮ | or Princess Tutu @ 800) 524 ▮ | or Princess Tutu @ 800) 524 ▮ | or Princess Tutu @ 800) 524 ▮ | or Princess Tutu @ 800) 524 ▮

Poster Five

lost animals, but in fact they merely come perilously close to the wrong target, which is one of the three ways to make edgy humor (see the Shock Funny Filter in *How to Write Funny*). At first sight, people who encounter the posters might be horrified by the cruelty, but as soon as they realize they're a joke, the real Subtext (people aren't adequate stewards of animals) would squeak through for most readers.

Ricardo did indeed hang the posters around town. He received a few

FOUND.
DELICIOUS.

FOUND AT BRYN MAWR & SHERIDAN. SMALL FEMALE OF MIXED BREED TASTED DELIGHTFUL WITH SOME ROASTED POBLANO AIOLI. DOG TAG SAID 'NALA' CALL ME (312) 869-4435

Poster Six

calls from people who were concerned. The calls went to his voicemail, and he planned to play the messages on a podcast, making for a daring and original street art experiment that had potential to get noticed.

The calls were funny, but in the end, he didn't get enough of them to work with, so he abandoned the project.

However, he learned a lot from the experience, and went on to do other professional writing, including a piece in "Shouts & Murmurs." These

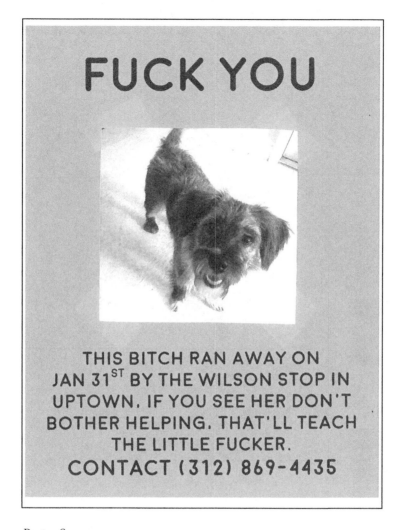

Poster Seven

posters make a nice portfolio piece that set him apart from other writers for his originality and edginess.

MISSING

SHITMACHINE

RAN AWAY NEAR WRIGLEY FIELD
ON FEBRUARY 3RD AT 2PM. GOES BY
NALA. SMALL MIXED BREED WITH
BLACK HEFTY SHITS.
CONTACT (312) 869-4435

Poster Eight

Poster Nine

EXAMPLE 5:
WATERBOARD YOUR CHILD

I asked Matthew Prager to write an article for *Blaffo*. The pre-selected title I gave him was "Waterboard Your Child To Better Grades," a joke headline by David Harden-Warwick.

The riffing notes he got from me and a small feedback group were sparse:

- a helpful how-to feature, sort of like a back-to-school article
- "My son used to get all B's but then I waterboarded him and now he get's A's and refuses to speak!"
- Also works for dogs

Here's Matthew's first draft:

WATERBOARD YOUR CHILD TO BETTER GRADES

We all love our children and want nothing more than for them to succeed. And nothing is more frustrating than seeing them fail to thrive in the way you know they should. And you've tried to help: you've screamed at them, you've shouted at them, you've even yelled at them, but nothing seems to work right?

That's how it was with my Caleb, that is until I discovered the ancient art of waterboarding. Thanks to waterboarding, Caleb is doing better in school, treating me with respect and showing absolute obedience to authority.

Waterboarding has a rich and fascinating history, from the Khmer Rouge to the good ol' USA and that's because it works. Waterboarding is a proven, effective way to change behavior. And the best part is you can waterboard your child right in your own home with products you already own!

All you need to do is lay your little guy down on his back, put a cloth over his mouth and pour water over the cloth for a period of 20 to 40 seconds. I like to use a terrycloth, but feel free to experiment! Half the fun of waterboarding is finding your own unique technique which reflects your values as a mother and an individual.

If you need help restraining your child, that's OK. Even experts find it difficult to waterboard a child over 6 alone. In fact it's a great excuse to get your hubby involved in the action to hold the little munchkin down. You can also get any other siblings involved too if they get jealous not being the center of attention. Have them say the countdown or hold down one spasmodic limb. Waterboarding is so effective that just being the room when it happens can help unruly children settle down, so get the whole family involved.

And don't worry if your child seems upset or begins to cry, that's means the waterboarding is working. Remember your child only feels like they're drowning so don't be misled by those crocodile tears!

You will not believe the results. Only one or two sessions can be all it takes to correct negative behavior. Before waterboarding, my Caleb was constantly talking back, but just three sessions later and he hasn't said a word to me in months. Talk about night and day.

Of course, once you've tried waterboarding once, you'll of course want to jazz it up a little bit. I like to make waterboarding into an educational experience by using Spanish vocabulary. Inquisitors called waterboarding tortura del agua, and now that's what my kids call it too. You should have seen how impressed their Spanish teachers were!

And why stop with your children? Just about anyone can benefit from waterboarding whether it's a spouse, a flakey friend, or a total stranger who just stole your parking space. Of course advanced waterboarding comes with its own set of challenges, but by this time you're an expert and ready to waterboard just about anyone.

Here are the notes I gave him:

> "The article needs to escalate more. It seems to pretty much be on the same pitch throughout. I recommend not using first person, but rather a magazine feature voice. That way you can interview some CIA black-site torturer as if he's an education expert or something, because such articles always have an expert quoted. The whole trick here is contrast—see how horrifying and scary you can get with the details and yet how normalized you can make it sound in the way you talk about it. Contrast things we associate with comfortable middle class parenting and helping kids with homework with super dark torture."

He thanked me for the feedback, then gave me this second draft a few days later:

WATERBOARD YOUR CHILD TO BETTER GRADES

Everyone loves their children and wants nothing more than to see them succeed. And equally nothing is as frustrating as seeing them fail when they should be thriving. You've tried screaming, you've tried yelling, you've even tried shouting: nothing seems to work! But have you tried waterboarding?

Waterboarding has a rich and fascinating history, from the Khmer Rouge to the good ol' USA and that's because it works. Waterboarding is a proven, effective way to change behavior. And the best part is you can water-board your child right in your own home with products you already own!

All you need to do is lay your little guy down on his back,

put a cloth over his mouth and pour water over the cloth for a period of 20 to 40 seconds. Many experts recommend a terry-cloth, but feel free to experiment! Half the fun of waterboarding is finding your own unique technique which reflects your values as a mother and an individual.

If you need help restraining your child, that's OK. Even experts find it difficult to waterboard a child over 6 alone. In fact it's a great excuse to get your hubby involved in the action to hold the little munchkin down. You can also get any other siblings involved too if they get jealous not being the center of attention. Have them say the countdown or hold down one spasmodic limb. Waterboarding is so effective that just being the room when it happens can help unruly children settle down, so get the whole family involved.

We also recommend waterboarding your tyke on a plastic tarp to avoid any unnecessary clean-up. After a hard waterboarding session there's nothing worse than having to clean up vomit or urine out of your brand-new carpet!

And don't worry if your child seems upset or begins to cry, that is just the waterboarding working its magic. Remember your child only feels like they're drowning so don't be misled by those crocodile tears!

Of course, once you've tried waterboarding once, you'll of course want to jazz it up a little bit. I like to make waterboarding into an educational experience by using Spanish vocabulary. Inquisitors called waterboarding tortura del agua, and now that's what my kids call it too. You should have seen how impressed their Spanish teachers were!

Frankly there is no good reason not to water-board your little prince or princess. Don't take our word for it, many experts now saying that waterboarding should be right in every parent's handbook alongside time-outs and an allowance.

According to Mr. Jones, a CIA station chief in [REDACTED],

Romania, you're not parenting right if you're not waterboarding. "Waterboarding is bar none, the best psychological weapon we have providing maximum pain with minimal to no permanent physical damage." Mr. Jones says it doesn't matter how stubborn the subject is, with waterboarding they'll tell you what you need to know. Parents with withholding teens, take note.

And why stop with your children? Just about anyone can benefit from waterboarding whether it's a spouse, a flakey friend, or a total stranger who just stole your parking space. Of course advanced waterboarding comes with its own set of challenges, but by this time you're an expert and ready to waterboard just about anyone. So get out there and remember, have fun!

My notes on his second draft:

"This one needs a lot of work. It reads too much like an ad. It needs to be more serious, with studies showing the effectiveness. The jokes will come in the contrast between respectable educators doing research and kids screaming for air. I think you show too much Subtext here by mentioning the CIA and such."

This feedback must have been frustrating to get. I didn't like the CIA mention, yet I was the one who suggested he bring the CIA into the picture! This can sometimes happen with feedback. As with the writer, sometimes a beta reader doesn't know whether something will work until they see it. Nonetheless, he kept at it and produced this draft:

Waterboard Your Child To Better Grades

Everyone loves their children and wants nothing more than to see them succeed. And equally nothing is as frustrating as seeing them fail when they should be thriving. Parents are always searching for a better way to discipline their children. And that's why many of them have turned to waterboarding.

Waterboarding has a rich and fascinating history, from the Khmer Rouge to our very own United States, and that's because it works. Waterboarding is a proven, effective way to change behavior. Frankly there is no good reason not to water-board your little prince or princess. Don't take our word for it, many experts now saying that waterboarding should be right in every parent's handbook alongside time-outs and an allowance.

"In a longitudinal study with 800 children, we found that waterboarding is, bar none, the most effective method of altering behavior in children," says child psychiatrist Dr. Greg Kunstler of Harvard Medical School. "Whether in improving a child's study habits or simply making them more obedient to authority figures, waterboarding is king at producing positive behavioral change."

Experts find waterboarding so effective because it efficiently stimulates the human drowning reflex, pouring a steady stream of water into the child's mouth and nose, while at the same stopping just short of drowning. Unlike other more traditional methods of physical disciplining, waterboarding provides no risk of permanent physiological damage.

Waterboarding is so potent that researchers like Dr. Kunstler say its effects can linger months and even years after the last bout of waterboarding. "Parents who have waterboarded in the past have found that even mentioning the word, 'waterboard' can immediately change a child's behavior," notes Dr. Kunstler. "Something as simple as water draining from a faucet can send a previously moody child into a paroxysm of rigid obedience."

Other experts have found that waterboarding can also positively affect siblings and other family. "We found that exposing children, between 5 and 10-years-old, to footage of other children, adults and animals being waterboarded made them more manageable in the eyes of their parents," says Dr. Erin Tsu from John Hopkins. "The effect was even stronger when the children were shown waterboarding in person, or if the waterboardee was someone they knew like a friend or sibling."

While waterboarding is safe when done correctly, even proponents like Dr. Kunstler recommend the procedure be undertaken with care. "Be careful to waterboard for no more than 25 to 30 seconds, in the heat of the moment it is easy to lose track of time," warns Dr. Kunstler, "if the child stops struggling and screaming, they've lost consciousness." Thankfully that problem comes with an easy fix: simply laying the child on their side and slapping their back should have the conscious and ready to be disciplined for that tantrum in no time.

Many doctors and child behaviorists also note that waterboarding is applicable to children of all ages. A 2004 Stanford Study found that whether they're a nearly adult teen or just four-years-old, all children equally fear the sensation of drowning. It's no wonder that some child behaviorists now say that waterboarding is going to be the next big parenting phenomena.

I accepted this draft and told Matthew I'd do some editing. I thought it was in serviceable shape. Here's what I published:

WATERBOARD YOUR CHILD TO BETTER GRADES

Parents are always searching for more effective and less traumatizing ways to discipline children and encourage good behavior. That's why many parents today have turned to waterboarding.

Waterboarding has a rich and storied history in education, from the Khmer Rouge to our very own United States, and that's because it works. Waterboarding is a proven, effective way to change behavior. Many experts are now recommending waterboarding be a tool in every parent's toolbox, alongside positive discipline, time-outs, and allowance.

"In a longitudinal study with 800 subjects, we found that waterboarding is, bar none, the most effective method of altering behavior in children," says child-interrogation expert Abu Domi Saquaan from Saudi Arabia's Allah Medical School. "Whether in improving a child's study habits or simply making them more unquestioningly obedient to authorities such as teachers, interrogators or Imams, waterboarding is very effective at producing positive behavioral changes."

Waterboarding can come to the aid of young people struggling to maintain productive homework habits primarily for its unique ability to stimulate the human drowning reflex. By simply pouring a steady stream of water into a child's mouth and nose through a suffocating towel or cloth, parents can unlock a new layer of cooperation and productivity in their children.

Said one mom, Karen Witteger of Akron, OH. "Unlike other more traditional methods of physical disciplining, waterboarding fits my lifestyle because it has no risk of permanent physical damage."

Waterboarding is so potent that researchers like Dr. Allen Kunstler of the U.S. National Security Administration say its effects can linger months and even years after the last bout of waterboarding. "Parents who have waterboarded in the past have found that even mentioning the word, 'waterboarding' can immediately change a child's grades," Dr. Kunstler says. "Something as simple as the sound of water pouring from a faucet can send a previously moody child into a paroxysm of rigid attention to schoolwork."

Other experts have found that waterboarding can positively affect siblings and other family as well. "We found that exposing children between 5 and 10 years old to footage of other children, adults or animals being waterboarded made them more manageable," says Dr. Erin Tsu from John Hopkins University.

"The effect was even stronger when the children were held in the same basement area as the target, or if the waterboardee was someone they knew, liked, or otherwise did not want to see killed."

While waterboarding is safe when done correctly, proponents like Dr. Kunstler recommend the procedure be undertaken with care. "Waterboard for no more than 25 to 30 seconds," warns Dr. Kunstler, "If the child stops struggling and screaming, you have gone too far."

INFANT WATERBOARDING

Many doctors and child behaviorists note that waterboarding can be effective with children of all ages. A 2004 Stanford tudy found that even with infants to those up to 4-years-old, waterboarding can be a useful aid in eating right, going to bed on time, even behaving in public.

Johnson & Johnson has announced the release of a portable waterboarding kit for parents. The unit attaches to infant car seats, converting them instantly to a waterboarding platform. "I don't like to resort to turning on the digital devices like a phone or a DVD player in the card to get my kids to behave," Witteger says. "Now I have another tool."

For all its potential to make the lives of parents easier, waterboarding, according to Dr. Kunstler, could soon see a surge of adherents. "I believe this harmless technique will soon be in widespread use not just in international affairs, as we see it now, but it in our homes, schools, and places of worship in the years to come."

Matthew delivered good joke beats and a nice overall lack of awareness. I took his escalation further with the section on infant waterboarding, which he suggested in his line about waterboarding being effective for all ages. I also added specificity, and increased contrast and verisimilitude where I could.

EXAMPLE 6:
DECORATIVE GOURD SEASON

Collin Nissan wrote a Shock-ridden piece and sent it to *McSweeney's* editor Chris Monks. The piece came in in good shape, but from their email exchange, you can see how Chris drilled in on two of the principles we've talked about in this book to tweak the piece:

> TO: websubmissions@mcsweeneys.net
>
> FROM: Colin Nissan
>
> SUBJECT: Submission - Gourd Season
>
> Hi Chris, I'm not sure what your stance is on excessive swears, but this one is riddled with them. I thought I'd send it along anyway to see what you thought.
>
> Thanks for taking a look.
>
> Colin

IT'S DECORATIVE GOURD SEASON, MOTHERFUCKERS.

By Colin Nissan

I don't know about you but I can't wait to get my hands on some fucking gourds and arrange them in a horn-shaped basket on my fucking dining room table. That shit is going to look so goddamned seasonal. I'm about to head up to the attic right now to find that wicker cocksucker, dust it off and jam it with an insanely ornate assortment of shelacked vegetables. When my guests come over it's gonna be like, blammo! Check out my shellacked fucking decorative fucking vegetables, assholes. Guess what season it is? It's fucking Fall. There's a goddamned nip in the air and my house is full of mutant fucking squash.

I may even throw some multi-colored leaves into the mix, all haphazard like a crisp October breeze just blew through and fucked that shit up. Then I'm going to get to work on making a beautiful fucking gourd necklace for myself. People are going to be like, Aren't those gourds straining your neck? And I'm just going to thread another gourd onto my necklace without breaking their gaze and quietly reply, It's fall, dickheads. You're either ready to reap this freaky-assed harvest or you're not.

Carving orange pumpkins sounds like a pretty fucking fitting way to ring in the season. You know what else does? Performing a fucking all-gourd reenactment of an episode of Different Strokes – specifically the one when Arnold and Dudley experience a disturbing brush with sexual molestation. Well, this shit just got real, didn't it? Felonies and gourds have one very fucking important commonality. They're both extremely fucking real. Sorry if that's upsetting to you, but I'm not doing you any favors by shielding you from this shit anymore.

The next thing I'm going to do is carve one of the longer gourds into a perfect replica of the fucking Mayflower as a shout-out to our Pilgrim forefathers, then I'm going to do lines of blow off its hull with a hooker until the sun comes up. Why? Because it's not summer, it's not winter and it's not spring. Grab a calendar and pull your fucking heads out of your asses.

Have you ever been in an Italian deli with salamis hanging from their ceiling? Well then you're going to fucking love my house. Just look where you're walking or you'll get KO'd by the gauntlet of mishapen, zuccini-descendant bastards swinging from above. And when you do, you're going to hear a very loud, very stereotypical Italian laugh coming from me. I fucking warned you.

But right now all I want to do is kick back and thumb through Martha Stewart's Fall issue. That crazy bitch has some mind-blowing pinecone crafts in there that I plan on enjoying a really fucking confusing Autumnal tug session to.

McSweeney's editor Chris Monks responded:

TO: Colin Nissan

FROM: McSweeney's Web Submissions

SUBJECT: RE: Submission - Gourd Season

Hi, Colin -

I think this is funny, but it might funnier if the voice was a tad less crude. Most of the fuckings are fine, but the masturbation line at the end sort of turns him into more of a degenerate than he really needs to be. I think a guy so into decorative gourds that he drops F-bombs left and right is funny enough. Anything more and he comes off too abrasive.

So if you're up to tinkering with the ending a little, have at it and send it back.

Best,

Chris

Colin replied:

TO: websubmissions@mcsweeneys.net

FROM: Colin Nissan

SUBJECT: Gourds Redux

Hi Chris, thanks for saving me from myself there. Something felt wrong about this one and I think masturbation was the problem. It definitely got creepy.

Anyway, I tried a different ending, let me know what you think of this one.

Thanks Chris,

Colin

It's decorative gourd season, motherfuckers.

By Colin Nissan

I don't know about you but I can't wait to get my hands on some fucking gourds and arrange them in a horn-shaped basket on my fucking dining room table. That shit is going to look so goddamned seasonal. I'm about to head up to the attic right now to find that wicker cocksucker, dust it off and jam it with an insanely ornate assortment of shelacked vegetables. When my guests come over it's gonna be like, blammo! Check out my shellacked fucking decorative fucking vegetables, assholes. Guess what season it is? It's fucking Fall. There's a goddamned nip in the air and my house is full of mutant fucking squash.

I may even throw some multi-colored leaves into the mix, all haphazard like a crisp October breeze just blew through and fucked that shit up. Then I'm going to get to work on making a beautiful fucking gourd necklace for myself. People are going to be like, Aren't those gourds straining your neck? And I'm just going to thread another gourd onto my necklace without breaking their gaze and quietly reply, It's fall, dickheads. You're either ready to reap this freaky-assed harvest or you're not.

Carving orange pumpkins sounds like a pretty fucking fitting way to ring in the season. You know what else does? Performing a fucking all-gourd reenactment of an episode of Different Strokes – specifically the one when Arnold and Dudley experience a disturbing brush with sexual molestation. Well, this shit just got real, didn't it? Felonies and gourds have one very fucking important commonality. They're both extremely fucking real. Sorry if that's upsetting to you, but I'm not doing you any favors by shielding you from this shit anymore.

The next thing I'm going to do is carve one of the longer gourds into a perfect replica of the fucking Mayflower as a shout-out to our Pilgrim forefathers, then I'm going to do lines of blow off its hull with a hooker until the sun comes up. Why? Because it's not summer, it's not winter and it's not spring. Grab a calendar and pull your fucking heads out of your asses.

Have you ever been in an Italian deli with salamis hanging from their ceiling? Well then you're going to fucking love my house. Just look where you're walking or you'll get KO'd by the gauntlet of mishapen, zuccini-descendant bastards swinging from above. And when you do, you're going to hear a very loud, very stereotypical Italian laugh coming from me. I fucking warned you.

For now, all I plan to do is throw on a flannel shirt, some tattered overalls and a floppy fucking hat and stand in the middle of a cornfield for a few days. The first crow that tries to land on me is going to get his gloomy avian ass bitch-slapped all the way back to summer.

Welcome to autumn, fuckheads!

TO: Colin Nissan

FROM: McSweeney's Web Submissions

DATE: 9/17/09

SUBJECT: RE: Gourds Redux

This version works for me. My only suggestions is to say "that wicker fucker" instead of "that wicker cocksucker." To me that rolls off the tongue a little better. Plus, I like how the only real expletive he uses is fuck or variations of fuck. Actually, with that in mind, maybe he should say "It's fall, fuckos" instead of "dickheads" at the end of the second paragraph.

  - c

TO: websubmissions@mcsweeneys.net

FROM: Colin Nissan

DATE: 9/17/09

SUBJECT: RE: Gourds Redux

Sounds good to me. I changed the wicker line. How do you feel about "fuckfaces" instead of "fuckos?" - there's something I like about that for some reason. I dropped it in there, but feel free to change it, of course.

(I think this email exchange might be getting funnier than the essay...)

Thanks Chris

- Colin

IT'S DECORATIVE GOURD SEASON, MOTHERFUCKERS.

By Colin Nissan

I don't know about you but I can't wait to get my hands on some fucking gourds and arrange them in a horn-shaped basket on my fucking dining room table. That shit is going to look so goddamned seasonal. I'm about to head up to the attic right now to find that wicker fucker, dust it off and jam it with an insanely ornate assortment of shelacked vegetables. When my guests come over it's gonna be like, blammo! Check out my shellacked fucking decorative fucking vegetables, assholes. Guess what season it is? It's fucking Fall. There's a goddamned nip in the air and my house is full of mutant fucking squash.

I may even throw some multi-colored leaves into the mix, all haphazard like a crisp October breeze just blew through and fucked that shit up. Then I'm going to get to work on making a beautiful fucking gourd necklace for myself. People are going to be like, Aren't those gourds straining your neck? And I'm just going to thread another gourd onto my necklace without breaking their gaze and quietly reply, It's fall, fuckfaces. You're either ready to reap this freaky-assed harvest or you're not.

Carving orange pumpkins sounds like a pretty fucking fitting way to ring in the season. You know what else does? Performing a fucking all-gourd reenactment of an episode of Different Strokes – specifically the one when Arnold and Dudley experience a disturbing brush with sexual molestation. Well, this shit just got real, didn't it? Felonies and gourds have one very fucking important commonality. They're both extremely fucking real. Sorry if that's upsetting to you, but I'm not doing you any favors by shielding you from this shit anymore.

The next thing I'm going to do is carve one of the longer

gourds into a perfect replica of the fucking Mayflower as a shout-out to our Pilgrim forefathers, then I'm going to do lines of blow off its hull with a hooker until the sun comes up. Why? Because it's not summer, it's not winter and it's not spring. Grab a calendar and pull your fucking heads out of your asses.

Have you ever been in an Italian deli with salamis hanging from their ceiling? Well then you're going to fucking love my house. Just look where you're walking or you'll get KO'd by the gauntlet of mishapen, zuccini-descendant bastards swinging from above. And when you do, you're going to hear a very loud, very stereotypical Italian laugh coming from me. I fucking warned you.

For now, all I plan to do is throw on a flannel shirt, some tattered overalls and a floppy fucking hat and stand in the middle of a cornfield for a few days. The first crow that tries to land on me is going to get his gloomy avian ass bitch-slapped all the way back to summer.

Welcome to autumn, fuckheads!

TO: Colin Nissan
FROM: McSweeney's Web Submissions
DATE: 9/17/09
SUBJECT: RE: Gourds Redux
Fuckfaces works for me. I love fuckfaces. Fuckfaces is perfect.
Will post this next month sometime, before gourd season ends.
 - c

The simple tweaks Chris suggested to the piece tempered the Shock, which is almost always a good idea. One of the central rules of Shock is to use it in moderation. But he suggested modifying it in a specific way: to keep the take laser focused on one narrow track: juxtaposing quaint fall gourd decorations primarily with variations on the work "fuck," at least as far as the harshest swears go. This is a good example of maintaining joke discipline by staying strictly on the thin track promised by the title.

The Character in this piece is a big part of the humor. It's an ironic character with extreme contrast. As the piece progresses Colin introduces the Madcap element, introducing non sequitur wackiness as well as escalating the Shock in an innovative way, mentioning the molestation episode of *Diff'rent Strokes* performed by gourds, for example.

The piece became one of *McSweeney's* most-read stories.

EXAMPLE 7: HAPHAZARDLY SPLASHING HANDS

David Calkins wrote this fake-news piece:

CDC RECOMMENDS HAPHAZARDLY SPLASHING HANDS WITH WATER TO MAKE THEM FEEL CLEAN

Emphasizing the importance of disease prevention, the Director of the Center For Disease Control Tom Frieden urged Americans Tuesday to make sure their hands feel sufficiently clean by haphazardly splashing them with water after using the restroom.

"Making sure one's hands feel clean enough is one of the most important steps people can take to avoid spreading disease to others," said Frieden, who explained that the extra two or three seconds one spends moving their fingers back and forth under the faucet and indiscriminately shaking them off in the sink is all it takes to feel as if they've killed millions of disease-spreading bacteria.

"Whether you've been preparing food, using the restroom, or blowing your nose, the simple act of barely getting your hands wet and carelessly wiping them on your clothes is an effective

way convince yourself that you won't get anybody sick. As an
added measure, we recommend that people vigorously dry their
hands with three or four paper towels in order for their hands
to feel like they haven't been in close proximity to bodily fluids."

The director went on to clarify that people using public rest-
rooms need not take these measures if nobody else is watching.

The piece has good Subtext (the Government isn't trying anymore),
and it escalates the Reference Funny Filter by incorporating more relatable detail about poor hand-washing. Irony and Shock are also at play. It
stays on track with good joke discipline and has a nice button.

But a piece can always be improved. Here are my notes to him:

"Great job on this story. It's simple, tightly written, and escalates well. It's Irony and Reference, with clear Subtext. Submit
this somewhere! Or, if you want to take it to another level, you
could take the clue that since it's a heavily quoted piece from the
same character, you could rewrite it as CDC hand-washing in-
structions, using pretty much all the same Reference joke beats.
This would break you out of the *Onion*-style news-parody format and open you up to submitting to McSweeney's, Shouts &
Murmurs, or anywhere else you like. It would come across as
more original because it would be parodying something that
we haven't seen. If you play your cards right, the Subtext could
be the larger issue of deregulation under Trump. Whatever you
decide to do with it, good luck!"

David did as I suggested, rewriting the piece in a different format and
submitting it to *McSweeney's*:

DEREGULATED CDC HAND-WASHING GUIDELINES
1. Notice soap dispenser.
2. Wiggle fingers under faucet while counting to one.

3. Wipe bacteria on pants.

4. Omit 1-3 if others not present.

Here's the feedback he got from them:

"Piece is too short. Target and subtext are not clear. Feels like it's missing a punch. Not enough urgency, stakes not high enough."

David did a third draft, retaining his reworked title. Reworking a title is risky; it often results in the original joke being lost. But by aligning the title with his new format, he was able to at least set up the anticipation of the joke if not the joke itself, and most of his well-escalating joke beats survived:

Deregulated CDC Hand-washing Guidelines

As we prepare for deregulation under the new administration, we at the Center for Disease Control have revised our hand-washing guidelines for the general public. Americans are urged to take the following steps in order to prevent the spread of illness over the next four-to-eight years.

1. Wave fingers back and forth under faucet for roughly two seconds, or until hands feel clean, whichever happens sooner. Indiscriminately shake them off in the sink.

2. Carefully inspect hands and fingernails for millions of disease-spreading bacteria.

3. More serious diseases such as Salmonella, E. coli, and Norovirus, should be thoroughly wiped on pants.

4. If preparing food, handling diapers, or using the restroom, vigorously dry hands with paper towels* until contact with bodily fluids never happened.

5. Steps 1-4 may be omitted if nobody else is present.

* The deregulated EPA recommends no fewer than ten.

Here's the feedback he got:

"Target and subtext are clearer, but could be more specific. Try tying it to Trump's obsession with cutting business costs. Suggestion: work in a reference to the weird automated things you find in bathrooms. The asterisk at the end is distracting and confusing."

FUNNIER-WRITING TIP #17: A PIECE OF WRITING MUST HAVE A REASON TO EXIST

Why does your piece exist? You have to know the reason and be able to communicate it to the reader, overtly or otherwise. Either way, they need to feel that this is a story that must be told, and isn't just a waste of their time. News-parody articles need a news hook. Anecdotes need a "you have to hear this" quality to them. The reason to exist doesn't have to be real. It's a humor piece, so it's frivolous by nature. But a humor piece needs a sense of faux usefulness, a sense of fake urgency, or even just a first-person call to "please read this important message—I must get it out to the world!" The only mistake you can make in this regard is leaving the reader wondering, "Why should I be reading this?"

When two editors among his feedback group suggested tying the idea to the Trump administration, David made the wise decision to go that route. This gave his story relevancy, and a reason to exist. His next draft:

DEREGULATED CDC HAND-WASHING GUIDELINES

In preparation for more lenient regulations under the Trump administration, the Center for Disease Control is revising its official hand-washing guidelines. The CDC now recommends the following procedure for businesses aiming to recover time lost under previously stringent standards for hand hygiene.

1. Wave fingers back and forth under faucet for roughly two

seconds. Shake indiscriminately off in sink.

2. Immediately return to work if sink's motion sensor failed to wet hands, as that was the sink's responsibility.

3. Briefly check hands for millions of microscopic, disease-spreading bacteria. Omit this step if deep down you know you got them all.

4. More serious diseases such as Salmonella, E. coli, and Norovirus, may be wiped on pants.

5. Rationalize that at this point the use of soap would set you back too many steps.

6. If blowing nose or using the restroom, dry vigorously with paper towels until contact with bodily fluids never happened.

7. Steps 1-5 may be omitted if you are holding up an important conference call.

He got this feedback from *McSweeney's*:

"Target and subtext are clear now. Number 6 feels too similar to #3. Number 7 feels like a weaker out than the original. Reword and polish."

David did exactly that, and *McSweeney's* published his final piece:

Deregulated CDC Handwashing Guidelines
by David Calkins

Under the Trump Administration's more lenient regulations, the Centers for Disease Control are revising their official handwashing guidelines. The CDC now recommends the following procedure for businesses aiming to recover time lost under the previously stringent standards for hand hygiene.

1. Wave fingers back and forth under faucet for roughly two seconds. Shake off indiscriminately in sink.

2. Immediately return to work if sink's motion sensor failed

to wet hands, as that was the sink's responsibility.

3. Briefly check hands for millions of microscopic, disease-spreading bacteria. Skip this step if deep down you know you got them all.

4. More serious diseases such as salmonella, E. coli, and norovirus may be wiped on pants.

5. Rationalize that at this point the use of soap would set you back too many steps.

6. Steps 1-5 may be omitted if nobody else is present.

EXAMPLE 8: AN AFFAIR TO REMEMBER

Hugh Kelly began with this short story for a writing class:

AN AFFAIR TO REMEMBER

By: Hugh Kelly

Sitting on a beige couch with her right hand plastered on her forehead in defeat while her tender thumbprints tenaciously grapple with a jilted glass of Hillary Clinton circa 2016 Chardonnay, Annalise Anderson's furrowed brow and passive, nonchalant tears casually drip into her drink as she guzzles the anesthetic down her throat. Her shoulder length, relaxed jet-black hair, and cream-colored turtleneck along with her stylish slacks only serve to complement the sexually repressed tone of the living room she shares with her husband, Jasper. Jasper approaches his wife with the glitter of guilt plastered on his face idly making his way down the staircase.

"Hey," says Jasper as he sits on the couch next to his bereaved wife slowly as he oddly caresses the coiled backs of her hands with an unfamiliar touch. "I just wanted you to know…"

"Shut up, Jasper!" snaps Annalise. "You're a stupid, stupid son of a bitch. You're a stupid ungrateful bastard."

Jasper nods, "I know. I wish I didn't know what a perverse idiotic imbecile I am, but consequently, that is one of the few things I do know."

Annalise looks away from her husband, tears drying up; resonating in rage. Her head tilts forward as the incredulous, disastrous notions of her husband's "indiscretions" become clearer in her mind.

"How could you bring that trashy ass bitch in our house--in my house?" asks Annalise.

"Well, I--she--she just found me, she found us…" Jasper's attempt at stammering out a cohesive answer to his wife's allegations are met with only more muttered juxtaposition.

A crestfallen Annalise stares down Jasper, "How many times?"

Responding without hesitation, Jasper cracks a smirk, "I don't know, babe. Probably three times."

"In this house?!"

"Well, yeah, that's kind of what I just said, babe," replies a snarky Jasper. "Sahara and I were together a few times. Once at my office, once on our kitchen table, and once inside of a porta potty next to that Waffle House down the road. Oddly enough, the porta-potties provided the most discretion," replied Jasper.

Annalise stands in anger; the hairs on the back of her neck creep to a crescendo. She clutches her forehead as it feels as though it's going to blow up and splatter across the room as if it were an HBO miniseries.

"My friends, my family," says Annalise. "This whole judgmental upper-middle-class town knows. Now…Big Brother… even he knows."

Jasper nods as he stands to try to calm his pacing wife, "Yeah, I mean, and I didn't even realize that Agent Sahara was Big

Brother at first. I thought we were just going to have this casual, hot steamy sexual affair."

"Of course, Jasper, sex was the only thing that was supposed to happen in our open marriage," says Annalise. "I didn't realize you were going to plan the next wave of ISIS with some FBI informant. Baby, how could you fucking betray me like that?!

"Babe, I'm sorry," says Jasper. "It just happened. I don't know--I--it was just this emotional affair at first, then Agent Sahara started wanting more. A future together. A life. Tax withholding information"

As Jasper tries to caress his wife's shoulder, Annalise sharply rejects this, "DON'T TOUCH ME!"

"I'm sorry. I don't know how to make this up to you," pleads Jasper.

"I'll tell you how you're gonna make it up to me: You're gonna call that little FBI slut and you're gonna tell her to never gonna contact you ever again, Jasper!"

"It's not that easy. They've put little cameras around the house, they've wiretapped the phones," says Jasper. "Agent Sahara is even standing right outside that window watching us have this conversation."

Annalise looks over her shoulder as the loud, visceral tones of fear illicit themselves through shrieking screams. A tall, swarthy woman with long dark hair and a trench coat stands with a nearly flawless visage and FBI badge pressed against the stainless glass window.

"FBI, BITCHES!" blurts out Agent Sahara, the venerated member of the Bureau of nearly 15 years.

Annalise's face drops "Wait, hold up--hold up. Babe, is that her? For real?"

"Deadass, baby," says Jasper as he winces for verbal assaults from his wife and the actual physical assault looming on the horizon from the stealthy FBI agent outside his window.

"Oh, hmm, well, okay, whatever, I cannot even believe you're into that," says Annalise to a dumbfounded Jasper. "I mean, like, she's pretty or whatever, but she ain't all that."

Hugh's professor told him the flow of the story was good, but asked for more dynamics between the Annalise and Jasper characters, suggesting he show Jasper as more oblivious so the joke of the story lands harder.

My notes were similar. I told him he had potential with this idea, a good take, and good escalation. But I thought he needed more radical changes. I recommended he rewrite the piece as a script, since it's primarily dialog-based, and all the jokes are verbal or visual. His writerly descriptions do nothing to elevate the humor. In fact, they hinder it.

I suggested he begin it as a standard wife-yelling-at-husband-for-having-an-affair sketch, then quickly introduce the escalating beats, showing how much of a big betrayal this truly was. I advised him to keep it simple, focus on the joke, get rid of everything else, and end up with maybe 4–5 pages in standard script format.

He rewrote it. (See opposite page.)

I replied:

"I'm glad to see this rewritten as a script! However, you're using a format like a production script, which is overkill. Any sketch you submit for a TV show job should be in more of a spec format. Also, you still have far too much description, none of which is essential for understanding the action. You should use as little description as possible—that makes this a script more accessible. It's the director's job to figure out where people are sitting and how the scene is blocked, and a production designer's job to figure out what the set looks like, and a casting director's job to figure out who to cast. The writer's job is not to limit the work of those other crewmembers, but make their jobs easier by being more open to however they want to execute

VIDEO	AUDIO
INT. SUBURBAN UPSTATE NEW YORK HOUSE-LIVING ROOM-NIGHT:	
Sitting on a long, stately beautiful white couch with her legs plastered Indian style across it's countenance, ANNALISE ANDERSON, mid to late 30's, African-American, impeccably beautiful, stares forward with tears streamlining down her cheekbone.	
While her furrowed brow, contemplative eyes, and racing stream of consciousness grapple with something clearly tugging at her heart, Annalise's right hand is also grappling with one fatass glass of Chardonnay.	ANNALISE (mumbling to herself) I knew I should've cut his whole thing off when I had the chance.
Annalise takes one long, disturbingly extended of her glass of swine nearly swallowing it whole as it splashes down her facade.	
The Chardonnay dribbles down her face in an earnest attempt to take the place of the tears coming from her eye socket.	MALE VOICE (o.s.) Hey...
CRACK! The visceral sound of Annalise's neck cracking towards the sight of the offscreen voice is represented in the strange sound of pebbles colliding into one another.	

"An Affair to Remember" (first draft script, page 1).

it. Since this script is not in production, the concept should be presented in as clear a way as possible with no distractions. So, I recommend cutting ALL the description and just writing 'Typical suburban home.' Then go right into the dialog. Also, remove ALL actor direction (in parentheses before each line). That should almost never be used, for the same reason.

"I don't advise that you be precious with the dialog at this

VIDEO	AUDIO
The identity behind the voice is revealed as a man, Annalise's husband, JASPER ANDERSON, also African-American and also mid to late 30's, makes his way down the staircase. His hand--primarily and oddly enough his ring finger--tremble with a tenacity that outweighs it's sincerity and perceived loyalty.	ANNALISE (after a brief glimpse of her approaching husband; tears welling in her eyes) Oh, Dear God!
With the quickness, Annalise grabs the bottle of Chardonnay that was resting on the coffee table adjacent to her. She pours the remainder of the contents inside her empty wine glass.	
A little too much of its contents. So much so that the wine begins spilling in large quantities--a waterfall wine parade, in fact--out of Annalise's glass and onto her $4,000 carpet.	
Jasper takes a solemn seat next to his wife as she downs most of her drink while doing everything she can to avoid eye contact.	JASPER (awkwardly caressing Annalise's hand) Sweetheart, I-- ANNALISE --You bastard! Do not...TOUCH ME!
And with the flick of her empowered wrist, Annalise hurls her wine into Jasper's face. The only issue with that is Annalise had downed so much of her drink that only about half a tablespoon of wine actually manages to make contact with Jaspers face.	

"An Affair to Remember" (first draft script, page 2).

stage. Better to just hammer it out. The exact wording of lines is only important at the very end of the writing process, when the structure is nailed. And you still need to nail the structure.

"The main issue with the structure is that we need to know the 'game' of the scene earlier. You start it on page 4 now and that's way too late. We need to know that it's the unreal level of

3

VIDEO	AUDIO
After an awkward pause, Jasper condescendingly dabs the scant amount of wine off of his cheek.	JASPER I guess I deserved that. ANNALISE (angry crying) Shut up, Jasper! You're a stupid, stupid son of a bitch! I should have never married you. You're a stupid, ungrateful bastard! JASPER I know, honey. I-I wish I didn't know what a perverse, idiotic imbecile I am, but consequently, that is actually one of the few things I do know.
Annalise's breathing turns into fumes as her tears begin to dry up. She stares upwards towards the ceiling before looking her husband dead in the eye.	ANNALISE How could you do it? How could you bring that trashy ass hoe up in our house--up in my house?! JASPER Well, I--she just found me--I--she found us. ANNALISE How many times? JASPER We did it three times. In the dining room. With your vibrators. ANNALISE In this house?! JASPER Yeah, sweetheart, that's kinda', like, what I just said.
Annalise stands up forcefully in response to her husband's snark.	ANNALISE Don't you be smart with me, you 35-year-old bedwetter!

"An Affair to Remember" (first draft script, page 3).

Jasper's betrayal that's escalating: first an affair, then we find out the person he had the affair with was a spy and he shared state secrets, then we find out he betrayed the whole country (maybe it could then escalate to him betraying the whole planet?). It needs to keep getting more exaggerated on a track like this until we find out the house is surrounded and everyone's gonna get

4

VIDEO	AUDIO
Jasper stands following his wife's suit, but in a calmer, almost demeaning manner in an attempt to soothe her justifiable rage.	JASPER Babe, I don't know what to say. Sahara and I were only together a few times. Once in my office, once on our kitchen table, and, like, ten times in that porta-potty next to that Waffle House down the road. (beat) Who would have thought that porta-potty would have provided the most discretion?
Annalise paces back and forth between the living room and the large window behind both her and Jasper. The storm outside has gun trickling down harder; the thumping sound of the of the raindrops against the window is even more omnipresent in this moment.	ANNALISE (clutching her head) Oh, for God sake's, Jasper! You're a loser and a liar! My friends, my family, everybody in this shrillish, judgmental, upper-middle-class pill popping cesspool of a town knows. (swallows hard) Now...Big Brother...even he knows. JASPER (nervously gesturing) My bad, babe, I know. The thing is when I first met her, I just thought that we'd have this casual, hot, steamy sexual affair. I didn't know that Agent Sahara was that deadass. I didn't know she was actually Big Brother. ANNALISE Oh, she was definitely deadass, you dumbass!

"An Affair to Remember" (first draft script, page 4).

arrested. Your closer joke about the threesome will work quite well, but right now it's not played up with enough contrast. It will be funnier as a button on the scene if you heighten the betrayal that leads up to it.

"The way you're off from the game of the scene is by telling too many jokes that have nothing to do with the game. A

5

VIDEO	AUDIO
Jasper edges his wife back towards the couch away from the window in an attempt to get her to sit down and calm her. They sit clasped together only momentarily before Annalise angrily pulls away from Jasper standing with the brute of The Rock.	ANNALISE (CONT'D) Damn it, man! You were only supposed to be having sex outside of our marriage, not doing all this other extra nonsense. How could I have ever known that you were gonna' plan the next wave of ISIS with some FBI informant? Babe, how the hell could you betray us with such gravitas?! JASPER (standing again) It just happened! I can't even put into words--it was this emotional affair at first. Then, Agent Sahara started wanting more: A future together, a life, tax withholding information.
Without warning, Annalise suddenly throws up in anguish on Jasper's offscreen shoes. She picks herself up rather quickly as if her throwing up did not just happen and sits on the couch. Jasper sits beside her.	JASPER Oh, my God, babe! ANNALISE (trembling) It should have been in that treacherous ass mouth of yours. JASPER I'm sorry. I don't know how to make this up to you. ANNALISE I'll tell you what you're gonna do: You're gonna' call that little FBI slut, and you're gonna' tell her to never, ever contact you again--if only for multiple orgasms. JASPER I wish I could, but it's not that easy, babe. They've already put little cameras all over the house...there...
Jasper points to a microscopic camera hidden on a nearby tv remote.	JASPER(CONT'D) There...

"An Affair to Remember" (first draft script, page 5).

comedy piece like this should have one line of jokes. The first few lines of the script need to be the kinds of things people always say in these conversations, some of which you have right: things like, 'I can't believe you did this,' and 'how could you?' and 'I'm so sorry, I didn't mean to hurt you.' But not many lines. Just enough to establish the idea. All those jokes about

VIDEO	AUDIO
Jasper points to a microscopic camera on a framed picture of the couple smiling at an amusement park.	JASPER(CONT'D) Hell, there's even a camera there...
Jasper points to a microscopic camera planted on his wife's middle finger which stands firmly in Jaspers face.	ANNALISE Well, do something! Anything! Be a man! JASPER (starting to whimper heavily) I-I-I can't. It's too late for that! (points to the o.s. window) Look, Agent Sahara is standing right outside that window watching us have this entire conversation!
We whip pan sharply to reveal AGENT SAHARA, tall and swarthy, dark brown hair, nearly flawless visage, and to top it all off, a trenchcoat. She stands outside soaked from the rain with her FBI Badge pressed against the stainless glass window.	
The sound of Annalise screaming and a wine glass shattering to the floor are heard simultaneously.	AGENT SAHARA It's FBI, bitches! We have a warrant for treasonous criminal conspiracy against the United States and a second warrant for the possibility of a terrible threesome between me and your wife.
Annalise's face drops as she approaches the window with Jasper cowering behind her. Despite the shock and horror of the situation, there seems to be one unbeknownst thing driving Annalise's angst:	ANNALISE Wait, hold up, hold up. Babe, is that her? For real? JASPER (bracing for verbal assaults from his wife) Deadass, baby. Deadass.

"An Affair to Remember" (first draft script, page 6).

how many times they did it in the house and the vibrators and all that stuff is 'off take,' meaning it doesn't belong because it doesn't escalate the game of your scene, your main joke (how outlandish his betrayal is). Other lines that don't work and ring out like wrong notes: her insulting him for being a bedwetter; the porta potty joke; 'My friends, my family, everybody in this

```
                                                                    7
        ┌─────────────────────────┬──────────────────────────────┐
        │          VIDEO          │            AUDIO             │
        ├─────────────────────────┼──────────────────────────────┤
        │ A stink face spreads across │ ANNALISE                 │
        │ Annalise. A dumbfounded     │ Uh-huh, well, uh, okay, whatever. You │
        │ Jasper stares at his wife as│ know what, I cannot even believe you're │
        │ she stares at Agent Sahara. │ into all of that. I mean, she's pretty │
        │                             │ or whatever, but her nails are dusty, │
        │                             │ her shoes are dusty, and I see the │
        │                             │ outlines of a subway card from 1992 │
        │ THE END                     │ in her jean pocket. │
        └─────────────────────────┴──────────────────────────────┘
```

"An Affair to Remember" (first draft script, page 7).

shrillish, judgmental, upper-middle-class pill popping cesspool of a town knows"; 'I know, honey. I-I wish I didn't know what a perverse, idiotic imbecile I am, but consequently, that is actually one of the few things I do know' (this one, like a lot of the lines, doesn't sound like the way a real person would talk.) These lines are taking us down a wrong road, trying to be funny and make jokes that aren't related to the game of the scene. That's not how a sketch works. The jokes in a sketch (or any short comedy piece) need to be along the same track, the game of the scene. And the game here is about deepening just how far his betrayal goes. Once the audience knows this is a scene about a couple dealing with an affair, which will happen literally after the first 1-3 lines, then we need to have the fist beat of the joke, which the audience will identify because it will be the first unusual thing to happen in the scene. Everything prior to that will be typical, but then you introduce a strange element.

"You introduce the strange element in this draft with her line, "Now...Big Brother...even he knows." It's a mistake for her to be the one to introduce the game of the scene. It should be the man. It should be like a confession, with her getting more shocked each time he escalates the confession. He can simply refer to his mistress as "agent sahara." The woman will be taken aback by this, saying "what did you call her?" And then the man can explain that not only was she his secret lover, but she's also a spy working in secret against the interests of America. The woman can then spell it out: 'wait a minute, so you not only betrayed me, you betrayed the country?' (Remember, it's important to know what joke you're telling, and be sure your reader knows what joke you're telling.) If the man maintains the same sheepish, apologetic tone as when he first admitted the affair, that will be funny—he should be unaware that the more this escalates, the worse it is. Next, he should escalate by saying, 'I'm afraid it's worse than that.' Then he can admit that he gave her state secrets that will allow her to destroy the entire country or kill everyone in it. Now the woman is horribly shocked. Then keep building it so his betrayal is worse and worse. I suggest building to his betraying the whole planet. It's always good in comedy to build to the absurd. If space aliens are involved and they're going to enslave the entire human race and keep the women to work in the mines or in a barely-conscious state as a breeder female on some prison planet while the man escapes to a pleasure planet with his mistress, all the better. But it all needs to come back to "Sorry, babe, I didn't mean to hurt you." Him treating these big betrayals like they're mere indiscretions that he's sorry for will be increasingly funny. Use Analogy to map a regular affair onto this outrageous betrayal. Then end it with your threesome joke and you're good!

"This is minor, but I also recommend you change the character names to MAN and WOMAN. Again, this makes it more accessible and gives producers more flexibility. Be considerate of any producer who might want to produce this script, or any actors who might star in it. Make it easy to read, and don't be too demanding or rigid about how you envision it. Instead of 'tears welling in her eyes,' for example, just say 'crying' (or best yet, cut this direction entirely—you're not the director!)—most actors can't summon real tears, especially for a comedy sketch. Let them decide how to best perform it. That's just one example. All the direction and heavy description makes this script seem like it would be too much trouble to produce, and it gives the impression that the writer will be difficult to work with. Better to project a vibe that you're easy to work with!"

He came back with a second draft of the script. (See pages 186–191.) I replied:

"Basically, your changes didn't go nearly far enough. You don't quite have the script format down. Your description is way too long and there's way too much unnecessary information, description, and dialog throughout. You have to get rid of all that and cut to the chase. You need to get into to the meat of the conversation in the first couple of lines and start escalating. As is, you don't reveal any new information until the sec-

An Affair to Remember
By Hugh Kelly
September 21, 2018 (Version #1)

CAST
Man-30's
Woman-30's
Agent Sahara-late 20's

INT. TYPICAL SUBURBAN HOME—LIVING ROOM—NIGHT
A refined and elegant WOMAN, mid to late 30's, sits on her living room couch
with an ostensible state of sorrow and sadness dominating her mood. She downs
a fatass glass of Chardonnay as she stares forward blankly in rage. It is dark,
gloomy, and the sound of rain pouring excessively on a nearby window is heard
palpably.

                              WOMAN
                    I knew I should have cut his whole damn thing off when I had the
chance.
                              MALE VOICE
                    Hey...
An off-screen voice jolts Woman's attention (and the fierce sound her neck
cracking) towards an adjacent staircase. The voice belongs to the Woman's
husband, MAN. Man walks down the staircase and approaches his wife taking a
seat next to her as her body language rebukes his advances towards an intimate
embrace.
                              WOMAN
                    You Bastard! Drop dead!
                              MAN
                    Baby, I'm so sorry. I never, ever meant to hurt you like this. I
would never intentionally betray what we
                    had. It was just this big, ridiculous, stupid mistake.
                              WOMAN
                    Shut up, you moron! I should have never married you and your
                    stupid ungrateful ass. How could you do this to me? To us?
                              MAN
                    My bad.
The matter of fact tone of Man's further sets off his already irate wife.
                              WOMAN
                    God, you're such a narcissistic dirty pig. You never take anything
seriously, you never take any
                    responsibility for anything. You're always gaslighting literally
everything. Just be a man for once!

"An Affair to Remember" (second draft script, page 1).

ond page, and the audience is bored by that point. You're trying
too hard to inject jokes into this that are off-take. (like 'big ol'
sloppy penis,' 'Stormy Daniels of the FBI') — this only slows
you down. The only jokes you want in this piece are about how
absurd his betrayal is revealed to be, period.

"The characters still don't sound the way real people talk.

An Affair to Remember2

          MAN
I am a man, okay—with a big ole sloppy penis and everything! You
know that. What? You think I meant to destroy our marriage like
this. You think I like betraying our trust. It just—I don't know—it
happened so fast. And before I knew it...BOOM!

          WOMAN
I can't believe this. And what's even more cowardly of you is that
I'm the last to know about this. My family, my friends, this whole
freaking town. Everybody else knows about this little side-hoe of
yours.
          MAN
Yeah, babe, now Big Brother: even he knows.

Woman's expression winces in confusion/denial. She registers that her husband
has uttered the phrase "Big Brother" but she chooses to passively ignore it.
          WOMAN
        Stop it, okay. Just stop all this—whatever you're doing---and be
completely transparent with me. What
        went down?
          MAN
        It wasn't supposed to happen like this. It got so messy and
complicated. I mean, you and I had always
        mutually agreed that the only thing that was supposed to happen
outside of our marriage with
        strangers was, well, sex.
          WOMAN
Right.
          MAN
        So, when I first met her, I was only planning on having this hot,
steamy sexual thing, you know. But
        then it just kept escalating. I mean, we were only intimate
together, like, I don't know, a couple
        hundred times, so when it seemed like Agent Sahara started
wanting more, it completely caught me
        off guard.
          WOMAN
Wait a minute; what did you just call her?
          MAN
        Agent Sahara got super clingy super fast, bro. I couldn't help that.
It was just supposed to be this hot

"An Affair to Remember" (second draft script, page 2).

They sound very written. ('And what's even more cowardly of
you is that I'm the last to know about this.') This scenario is
well-known to the audience, we've seen it in a hundred movies
and TV shows. Get to it and show us the new and different part!
(the hyperbole of his betrayal). You introduce Big Brother before Agent Sahara. That's a mistake. You want the joke to esca-

An Affair to Remember3

tryst outside of my boring marriage, but then Agent Sahara wanted
more and more: A future together,   tax withholding
information, a new social security number and name for us in some far
away land.
                    WOMAN
          Huh.

                    MAN
          I'm telling you, babe, she got hella extra. How the hell was I
          supposed to know that my mistress was an FBI Agent using me to
          work against the interests of America?! I should have known all
          that by her head game?

After a loud scream after the true reveal of Man's betrayal, Woman hurls the
remainder of her Chardonnay in her husbands face before throwing the glass
behind her shattering it on the ground.
                    WOMAN
          You're telling me that you hooked up with the Stormy Daniels of
the FBI!
                    MAN
          She was so smooth, too. She got me to tell her my whole life story
          and all my disgusting secrets to her; spilling all my guts as I'm
          smashing her guts. It was guts on guts on guts everywhere!
                    WOMAN
          Wait a minute, you not only betrayed me, but the whole damn
          country?!

Man becomes even more sheepish and groveling than before. Almost begging.

                    MAN
          I'm so sorry, baby. I love you so much! I didn't want to break your
          heart. Please don't leave me!
                    WOMAN
          Stop it!
                    MAN
          It's worse than just the country, too. I gave Agent Sahara all the
          state secrets the D.O.D made me swear a blood oath protect. I told
          her about (bleep) and about our ski (bleep) (bleep) trip to Hawaii
          and I even told her about (bleep) and their attempts to infiltrate
          another Galaxy to (bleep) Mars.

"An Affair to Remember" (second draft script, page 3).

late and get bigger, not de-escalate. You want to start with Agent
Sahara and build to the whole government after that. Also, your
first joke beat takes too long. The man explains too much about
the affair with no new escalation.

"So, overall, this needs to be trimmed WAY down. The characters should say almost nothing. Just get to the point. Don't

An Affair to Remember4

The bleep's in parenthesis are meant to literally represent the sound of an FCC Censor bleep sound effect. This is followed by Woman immediately throwing up in shock all over Man's shirt.

                    WOMAN
          Oh, my God! Oh, my God!
                    MAN
          I can't believe it. I'm gonna' singlehandedly be responsible for
          every human female having to move to some weird breeder planet
          near Mars solely to be barely conscious, pimped out, and enslaved
          by...Alien Bros.
                    WOMAN
          And what? Look at me, you little punk! You just thought you'd run
          off to some hot new cosmopolitan planet with that little Agent
          Sahara?

Man hesitates slightly.
                    MAN
          Well, I hadn't thought of that, but now that you mention it.

Woman stands up assertively as she becomes more and more tired of her husbands blasé attitude towards his indiscretion

                    WOMAN
          I can't believe this. I'm leaving you.

Man stands up as well grabbing his wife's arm.

                    MAN
          Hold on, baby. Come on—what—you're overreacting. Lets go
          upstairs, watch a movie, and this'll all blow over. Or better yet, let's
          take a little night walk down the street to the bar and do some
          heavy drinking to solve these really insignificant problems. You
          know there are people starving somewhere.
                    WOMAN
          You have no sense of boundaries! Everything was going so stable,
          and you just had to sell the entire universe out with your wack ass
          emotional affair. Do you still love me?
                    MAN
          Yes, I do. I-I-I love you so much more than you could ever
    imagine. I will always love you. But I love
          Agent Sahara, too. And I wanted to explore other solar systems
          with her before I committed to anything real. I just didn't realize
          she'd have me committed something this freaking big so fast.

"An Affair to Remember" (second draft script, page 4).

worry about the characters not working or not being funny. Action is what makes character, not lines of dialog or descriptions of what wine they're drinking or whatever. And it's the comedic concept that will carry the piece, not all the detail that distracts from the concept. It also needs to be shorter and in proper script format."

An Affair to Remember5

WOMAN
I don't even believe this is happening. You are mentally ill.
MAN
Okay and...?
WOMAN
You have ruined our lives. I'm calling my lawyer in the morning. I want you to get you and all of your stuff the hell out of this house by tomorrow or so help me God! And! And! And! I want you to call that little Agent Sahara slutbag, and tell her to never contact you, me, or any human being as stupid as you ever again.
MAN
I wish I could, but it's not that easy, sweetheart. They've already hidden little cameras all over the house...there...

Man points to a microscopic camera hidden on a nearby tv remote.

MAN
There...

Man points to a microscopic camera on a framed picture of the couple at an amusement park.

MAN
Hell, there's even a tiny camera there...

Man points to a microscopic camera planted on his wife's middle finger, which stands up firmly in Man's face.

WOMAN
What the hell! What's going on? Do something. Do anything.
MAN
I can't. It's too late to do anything. Look, Agent Sahara is standing right outside that window watching
us have this entire conversation.

AGENT SAHARA, tall with dark brown hair, is revealed to be standing outside the large stainless glass window soaked from the downpour of the rainstorm. Her face is virtually smashed against the window as is her FBI badge. Both Man and Woman scream in unison at the reveal of Agent Sahara—this despite man being aware of the agents presence beforehand.

AGENT SAHARA
Freeze! It's FBI, bitches! We have a warrant for treasonous criminal conspiracy against America and
Planet Earth. Oh, and we also have a second warrant for the possibility of a terrible threesome
between me and your wife.

"An Affair to Remember" (second draft script, page 5).

An Affair to Remember6

THE END.

"An Affair to Remember" (second draft script, page 6).

He rewrote the script again, coming back with a third draft. (See pages 192–195.)

"AN AFFAIR TO REMEMBER" BY HUGH KELLY

Man and woman at home.

                    MAN
          Baby, I'm sorry.

                    WOMAN
          You bastard! You betrayed me!

                    MAN
          My bad, babe. See, what had happened
          was --

                    WOMAN
          That dumb skank--whatever her idiotic
          name is--what did she have that I
          didn't?

                    MAN
          Sweetheart, I never meant for things
          to go this far with Agent Sahara.

                    WOMAN
          Hold up, hold up! Uh, what did you
          just call her?

                    MAN
          She isn't exactly from this country.
          She needed me to show her our culture,
          and the contact information for our
          leading defense contractors, uh,
          locations of our missile silos,
          locations of all blast shelters. You
          know, stuff like that.

                    WOMAN
          What in the hell are you talking
          about?

                    MAN
          She wanted ALL the state secrets,
          baby.

                    WOMAN
          You narcissistic son of a bitch! How
          far did you actually take this thing?

                    MAN
          I'm sorry, honey. I don't want to keep
          secrets from you anymore. The invasion

"An Affair to Remember" (third draft, page 1).

2.

is supposed to happen Friday.

             WOMAN
What invasion?

             MAN
I messed up, baby. Forgive me.

         BULLHORN VOICE OUTSIDE
This is the FBI! The House is
surrounded!

OUTSIDE

Lots of noise outside: Cop car and fire truck sirens, guns
cocking, worried neighbors etc. are heard.

        SNOOTY NEIGHBOR OUTSIDE
I can't believe they're breaking up
like this; they were such a beautiful
couple. I told them marriage was hard
work. They didn't wanna' listen.

BACK INSIDE

Man and Woman have leaped to the floor to shield themselves
from the impending disaster.

             MAN
I told her everything about my work at
The State Department and how my bosses
were treating me like crap, and how
you weren't supporting me and so we
decided on this new world order and...

             WOMAN
Who plans The New World Order from
just one stupid ass one-night stand?!

             MAN
Hey, I didn't know my main mistress
was actually gonna' end up being a
sneaky ass Big Brother in disguise!
The future really is female.

             WOMAN
It's okay, baby, we've been through
worse. We can get through this. My
work friend told me about some good
couples counselors if we ever needed

"An Affair to Remember" (third draft, page 2).

3.

```
        it. And there's prescription pills for
        this sort of "thing, okay." We've got
        options!

Outside, the sounds of foreign Jetson style flying cars can
be heard along with the gasps of a crowd. Bright booming
lights, explosions, and general chaos can faintly be seen,
but definitely heard, in the distance outside.

                MAN
        Yeah, those options are being blown
        the hell up right now, baby. I can't
        save us: Big Brother has been watching
        us all this time. Literally! They
        planted these little cameras all over
        the house. There, there, and there!

Man points to a series of microscopic cameras hidden in tv
remotes, furniture etc; one is somehow planted on Woman's
middle finger, which is planted firmly in Man's face.

                WOMAN
        Why couldn't you have been honest with
        me? Why'd you have to go sneaking
        around behind my back?!

                MAN
        Cause she dumped me once she got
        everything she needed and planned it
        without me! She had me falling for her
        fast. That ass hole! Anyways,
        according to the NWO, all women are
        being mandated to move to Mars in 7 to
        10 business days. So, yeah, were very
        screwed. Sorry, my dude.

                WOMAN
        Boy, bye! You can run off to your
        little planet with Agent Sahara
        WITHOUT me. I'm leaving you, and so
        help me God if this isn't grounds for
        the biggest alimony payment this
        planet has ever seen!

Man begins behaving in a nearly possessed, rabid state after
Woman's last statement. Pleading, Man grabs Woman.

                MAN
        No! No! No! Agent Sahara promised me
        that there is no such thing as alimony
```

"An Affair to Remember" (third draft, page 3).

I complimented Hugh on making such drastic changes. Most second drafts aren't rewritten enough, and he rose to the challenge.

I told him this:

"The joke beats just need to be smoothed out and flow better, as well as clear up some confusing or overly wordy parts. I

```
                                                    4.

                on Mars. There is no alimony on mars!
                There is no alimony on MARS!

        Woman begins to stand but is startled by the sudden and very
        random presence of Agent Sahara herself standing right before
        them.

                        AGENT SAHARA
                Freeze! It's FBI, bitches! We have a
                warrant for treasonous criminal
                conspiracy against Planet Earth. Oh,
                and we also have a second warrant for
                the possibility of a terrible
                threesome between you, me, and your
                wife.

                        THE END.
```

"An Affair to Remember" (third draft, page 4).

wasn't getting the 'alimony on mars' beat. I think it's in line with the take for him to just be doing the standard male "sorry baby" like this is just a normal affair, for contrast."

With one final polish, Hugh produced a fourth draft. (See pages 196–199.)

"AN AFFAIR TO REMEMBER" BY HUGH KELLY

Man and woman at home.

                         MAN
               Baby, I'm sorry.

                         WOMAN
               You bastard! You betrayed me!

                         MAN
               My bad, babe. See, what had happened
               was --

                         WOMAN
               That dumb skank--whatever her idiotic
               name is--what did she have that I
               didn't?

                         MAN
               Sweetheart, I never meant for things
               to go this far with Agent Sahara.

                         WOMAN
               Hold up, hold up! Uh, what did you
               just call her?

                         MAN
               She isn't exactly from this country.
               She needed me to show her our culture,
               and the contact information for our
               leading defense contractors, uh,
               locations of our missile silos,
               locations of all blast shelters. You
               know, stuff like that.

                         WOMAN
               What in the hell are you talking
               about?

                         MAN
               She wanted ALL the state secrets,
               baby.

                         WOMAN
               You narcissistic son of a bitch! How
               far did you actually take this thing?

                         MAN
               I'm sorry, honey. I don't want to keep
               secrets from you anymore. The invasion

"An Affair to Remember" (fourth draft, page 1).

2.

is supposed to happen Friday.

                    WOMAN
          What invasion?

                    MAN
          I messed up, baby. Forgive me.

                    BULLHORN VOICE OUTSIDE
          This is the FBI! The House is
          surrounded!

OUTSIDE

Lots of noise outside: Cop car and fire truck sirens, guns
cocking, worried neighbors etc. are heard.

                    SNOOTY NEIGHBOR OUTSIDE
          I can't believe they're breaking up
          like this; they were such a beautiful
          couple. I told them marriage was hard
          work. They didn't wanna' listen.

BACK INSIDE

Man and Woman have leaped to the floor to shield themselves
from the impending disaster.

                    MAN
          I told her everything about my work at
          The State Department and how my bosses
          were treating me like crap, and how
          you weren't supporting me and so we
          decided on this new world order and...

                    WOMAN
          Who plans The New World Order from
          just one stupid ass one-night stand?!

                    MAN
          Hey, I didn't know she was gonna hurt
          me like this.

                    WOMAN
          It's okay, baby, we've been through
          worse. We can get through this.
          there's good couples counseling if we
          ever need it. We've got options!

Outside, the sounds of foreign Jetson style flying cars can

"An Affair to Remember" (fourth draft, page 2).

3.

be heard along with the gasps of a crowd. Bright booming
lights, explosions, and general chaos can faintly be seen,
but definitely heard, in the distance outside.

                    MAN
          Yeah, those options are being blown
          the hell up right now, baby. I can't
          save us: Big Brother has been watching
          us all this time. Literally! They
          planted these little cameras all over
          the house. There, there, and there!
          I'm so sorry, honey bun.

Man points to a series of microscopic cameras hidden in tv
remotes, furniture etc; one is somehow planted on Woman's
middle finger, which is planted firmly in Man's face.

                    WOMAN
          Why couldn't you have been honest with
          me? Why'd you have to go sneaking
          around behind my back?!

                    MAN
          Cause she dumped me once she got
          everything she needed! She had me
          falling for her fast. What happened is
          she sold us out to the rulers of the
          planet Mars, and all Earth women are
          being transported to Mars in 7 to 10
          business days. So, yeah, were very
          screwed. Sorry, my dude.

                    WOMAN
          Boy, bye! You can run off to your
          little planet with Agent Sahara
          without me. I'm leaving you, and so
          help me God if this isn't grounds for
          the biggest alimony payment this
          planet has ever seen!

                    MAN
          No! Baby, please. I messed up! It'll
          never happen again.

Woman begins to stand but is startled by the sudden and very
random presence of Agent Sahara herself standing right before
them.

                    MAN
          Agent Sahara?! Baby!

"An Affair to Remember" (fourth draft, page 3).

4.

```
                        WOMAN
              Baby! Oh, no you don't.

       She slaps him.

                        AGENT SAHARA
              Freeze! It's FBI, bitches! We have a
              warrant for treasonous criminal
              conspiracy against Planet Earth. Oh,
              and we also have a second warrant for
              the possibility of a terrible
              threesome between you, me, and her.

                        THE END.
```

"An Affair to Remember" (fourth draft, page 4).

Hugh took a sketch writing class during the process of reworking this piece, hoping to write more sketches for his portfolio.

EXAMPLE 9: CLAMS

Ian Harris came up with a list of 70 titles. With help from a feedback group of one, he chose "Clams are the sluts of the ocean" as the piece to write. I told him:

> "This is a magazine piece. Longer, and like a national geo-graphic article, but crazy-silly! Do it up!! Use of the word 'slut' is funny to me because it's so antiquated and sexist. ALL creatures in nature love sex."

Here's his first draft:

CLAMS ARE THE SLUTS OF THE OCEAN

The animal kingdom has left humanity with many mysteries but none more than the depths of the ocean. However, thanks to Depaul University's research team one such mystery, the clam, has been solved: unequivocally, clams are the sluts of the ocean. Indigenous the North America, Japan, Italy, and India for this hard shelled of a creature to reach the status of "slut" was a long time coming according to researcher, David Coyne. "Some creatures of the deep spend their entire lives and only copulate once, while others stay virgins their entire existence. Clams, however, go down on each other and perform oral sex acts almost immediately in coming in contact with another clam," said Coyne. According to Coyne, in some cases such clams haven't even exchanged how-do-you-do's before "doing" beings. It's worth noting that similar to other bottom feeders, clams are not Kosher leading 96% of clams to not be circum-cised. However, clam snipped penis or not, clams have been known to hop on and bang the shell out of each other until the tide goes out. "Although many animals enjoy sex," explained

Coyne, "it's the clam that performs sexual experiments on each other and engage in such acts as the Yummy Mummy, Dapper Danning, Superman Dat Hoe, and the New England Clam Chow'd That Pussy." Researchers hope to keep studying clams objectively but keeping getting too damn turned on themselves upon each trail study. "We have a lot to learn from our clam friends," said Coyne, "in order to receive further grant funding several staffers excitedly demonstrated a Superman Dat Hoe on myself to the Board of Education." Coyne and his researchers are still awaiting the Board's grant decision.

I replied:

"There's much to like here. The first bit and the last bit are the best. You lose your way in the middle a bit. I like the disparagement of clams as sluts, but it's less funny when they're personified. Funnier if sloppy undersea sex amongst clams is deemed by experts as slutty. Funnier if they're just calling clams sluts (and trollops and harlots and creatures of 'easy virtue') trying to be objective and conceal their sanctimonious attitude, but clearly judging the clams. And the madcap silliness is nice that you have going. The sex positions feel off-take. Funnier if it's about the researchers barely holding in their objections. And I think clams should have their own (or researchers came up with their own) names for clam sexual activities that aren't the same as human."

His second draft:

CLAMS ARE THE SLUTS OF THE OCEAN

The animal kingdom has left humanity with many mysteries but none more than the depths of the ocean. However, thanks to Depaul University's research team one such mystery, the clam, has been solved: unequivocally, clams are the sluts of the ocean. Indigenous to North America, Japan, Italy, and India in order for this hard shelled creature to reach the status of "slut" was a long time coming according to researcher, David Coyne. "Some creatures of the deep spend their entire lives and only copulate once, while others stay virgins their entire existence. Clams, however, perform floozy acts almost immediately in coming in contact with their kind," said Coyne. According to Coyne, in some cases such clams have been known to be downright minxes about how easy their virtue is. Furthermore, unlike other seas creatures who follow the laws of nature and decency, a trolloping-harlot seems to be the way of the clam . It is theorized but not yet proven, that clams seem to wear their bimbo-trampness as a badge of honor. "Although many animals enjoy sex," explained Coyne, "it's the clam that is such a whore they perform and engage in such sexual acts that are so inhuman we had to scientifically name them, such as: 'Tridacna Jugswipna','Trampna van Clampna', and 'Twointha Clamna Oneintha Stinkna.'" Researchers hope to keep studying the underwater-streetwalker objectively but keeping getting too damn turned on themselves upon each trail study. "In the end, we have a lot to learn from our loose friends in the sea," said Coyne, "in order to receive further grant funding several staffers excitedly demonstrated a 'Twointha Clamna Oneintha Stinkna' on myself to the Board of Education."

Coyne and his researchers are still awaiting the Board's grant decision.

My notes:

"This article isn't hitting the laugh button for me. The first was the wrong take but had more of a madcap feel. Also the slut synonyms are used oddly. Can you do one more pass that escalates the wackiness and insanity of this idea?"

His next draft:

CLAMS ARE THE SLUTS OF THE OCEAN

The animal kingdom has left humanity with many mysteries but none more than the depths of the ocean. However, thanks to DePaul University's research team one such mystery, the clam, has been solved: unequivocally, clams are the sluts of the ocean. Indigenous to North America, Japan, Italy, and India in order for this hard shelled creature to reach the status of "slut" was a long time coming according to researcher, David Coyne. "Although many animals enjoy sex," explained Coyne, "we watched clams have sex, and those acts were just inhuman, we scientifically named each act, such as: 'Tridacna Jugswipna','Trampna van Clampna', and 'Twointha Clamna Oneintha Stinkna.'" DePaul's researcher team's slut hypothesis was confirmed with careful reasoning and deduction. "Every moment of clam sex made hornier than a bull who's matador has fallen and can't get up," exclaimed Coyne, "however I did also want to vomit and shit at the same time." The laws of nature and decency clearly state that arousal plus disgust equals sluts. Coyne went on to explain that clams are the scientific equivalent of a frat boy with Viagra in his blood and 40 oz Bud Light Lime bottles for hands, one way or other he's going to pound over and over and over again, with a twist. "Imagine if Vanessa Carlton songs start to make sense, while having sex, and being possessed by a ghost. That's a clam that fucks, and it's slutty as shit," posits Coyne. Although possession is four fifths of the law one must wonder if clams are that last remaining fifth. Coyne and his team believe that clams are the key (and sluts) to future discoveries. The research team hopes to keep studying the slut objectively. Coyne's team have turned to each other to see such effects on humans, "Have my staff and I had an unadulterated clam orgy reenactment and streamed it on Twitch? YES, FOR SCIENCE!!" explained Coyne, "In fact, I asked our DePaul Board of Education if they'd perform 'Twointha Clamna Oneintha Stinkna' on me to see the importance of our findings."

Coyne and his researchers are still awaiting the Board's future funding decision.

Also, Vanessa Carlton was unavailable for comment.

My notes:

"Clams is still not working. It needs to be sillier. I started on a rewrite but realized I was re-writing too much trying to find a take, so you should do another pass. Be careful! 'for science' is a cliche. And I would avoid callback jokes in short articles. They're not long enough for those to work."

"Here's what I did with it, FYI...

"The animal kingdom has left humanity with many mysteries but none more than the depths of the ocean. However, thanks to North Carolina State University's research team one such mystery, the clam, has been solved. 'Clams are just crazy for clam cock,' according to lead researcher David Coyne.

"Indigenous to North America, Japan, Italy, and India, the hard shelled creature attained the status of 'sluts drunk on clam cum' after many years of empirically observed loose morals and wanton, spread-eagled depravity. Researchers have observed a shameless display of the clam laying prostrate before any suitor. 'Although many sea creatures enjoy sexual reproduction,' explained researcher David Coyne, 'as we observed clams reproduce, we found that there is nothing these tawdry whores won't try at least once, and probably more, because the gaping, jizz-slurping clam just can't get enough of the slutty clam-on-clam pounding it craves.'"

His next draft:

Clams Are The Sluts of The Ocean

The animal kingdom has left humanity with many mysteries but none more than the depths of the ocean. However, thanks to North Carolina State University's research team one such mystery, the clam, has been solved. "Clams are just crazy for clam cock," according to lead researcher David Coyne.

Indigenous to North America, Japan, Italy, and India, the hard shelled creature attained the status of "sluts drunk on clam cum" after many years of empirically observed loose morals and wanton, spread-eagled depravity. Researchers have observed a shameless display of the clam laying prostrate before any suitor. "Although many sea creatures enjoy sexual reproduction," explained researcher David Coyne, "as we observed clams reproduce, we found that there is nothing these tawdry whores won't try at least once, and probably more, because the gaping, jizz-slurping clam just can't get enough of the slutty clam-on-clam pounding it craves."

"The sexual acts of the clam were so inhuman that to study them we needed to name them," explained Coyne, "such as, 'Trapan van Clampna', 'Twointha Clamna Oneintha Stinkna', and 'Slooge Guzzling Clam.'" As each day passes researchers have witnessed clams continue to flagrantly experiment in newer and more truculent ways, "Some clams dig holes in the sand, fill the hole with cum, and jump in the cum hole and slut fuck," claimed researchers. With such new information regarding the clam a warning has been expressed by Coyne and his research team, "Nothing comes between a clam and it's sexual conquest, we've seen fish eviscerated and crabs beheaded in the name of clam pound town, proceed with caution because a clam wants it's unadulterated slut centric cum soaked penetration and it will get it."

My notes:

"Due to the nature of this idea, I think it needs another few graphs. I don't think the named sexual acts are particularly funny. This is really just a joke about a scientist being disgusted by sexual PDA in a clam, and yet observing it carefully. Also, the ascribing of human sexual peccadillos to clams. Maybe they tested talking dirty to clams? Or slapping the clam's ass during copulation—clams are turned on by EVERYTHING. They're sluts! That's your headline so that's what you have to escalate.

"Please write as much as you can and then it can be culled down. In fact, if you could spend like half an hour filling three pages with stream of consciousness nonsense and silliness for this, that would be perfect!"

Here's the stream-of-consciousness draft he wrote:

You name it clams are into it. The greater question is what doesn't turn clams on. Although the ocean has a lot of things inside of it it's things clams have never seen that still turn them on. A truck that fell off a ship, Air Supply albums, even random plans from a general contractor trying to rob a Wells Fargo that they came across—clams tried to fuck it. Ever see a clam riding another clam while trying to fuck a clam riding another clam? Researches have. Apparently it's common during storms as a end-of-days fuck.

It was found that all emotions for clams proceed horny. Scared clam moments later is a horny clam. Angry clam moments later is an angry honry clam. A horny clam moments later is a penetrating, being penetrated, or both.

Then there's the testing, researchers played Hoobastank music, made the clams watch the three Star Wars prequels and listen to a full four hour Glenn Beck broadcast—the clams? Still boned each other like nuts prior, during, and after. Researchers were sure the clams were affected but each variable put in front of the clams, but the clams didn't care. Clam disapproval ratings of the Star Wars films, due to brain waves, we're at an all time low of 2%. However the earth shattering sexcapades they had after and inspired by the Star Wars films were at 69% approval.

Several researchers injected the flu into clams to see if sickness would diminish the clams' ability to be constantly turned on. The clams used their flu induced vomit for lubricant. So researchers took all the clams away and left one clam alone by itself to see what it would do. Of course all the other clams were ignored and put in a bucket of brackish water that needed to be changed every 30 minutes due to the sheer jizzem load that was found in the bucket. The alone clam appeared to view the experiment as some some solitude sex gift and pleasured itself for six hours straight until it blacked out from exhaustion.

It is measured that a clam can produce half it's body weight in jizzem a day. And can swallow that amount in less than four seconds. It is estimated that 20% of a clams slimy body is jizzem from a past sexual encounter.

The clams were also left small whips and chains to see if BDSM would be an option for the clams. Having never come in contact with it they instead had sex with the whips and chain, and on them. Researchers don't know what this mean.

Researchers did attempt to slap the ass of a clam during sex which seemed to heighten the experience. Researchers were curious if it was possible for a clam mid sex to be sexing so hard that they'd kill another clam or itself by the sheer force of the pounding. Clams are estimated to take a psi of 42 before snapping in half. Amidst a nipple twisting moment during clam sex experience the two clams reached a psi of over 80 and exploded into each into blood, cum, and pearls. Other clams in the area immediately went to the floating blood, cum, pearl visage and fucked inside of it for several hours.

It should be noted that clams are constantly horny but not always having sex due to there not being other clams around. Although clams masturbate at a 3 per hour ratio, often clams will try to mate with other animals and creatures. Several sailors have been seduced by clams and lived to tell the tale. "Yeah, I fucked a clam once," said Jerry Makut, "I tell that story in bars constantly no one believes me...or wants to talk to me after I tell it. But I done it!"

Researchers have witnessed what appear to be signals from one clam to another that they are in fact in the mood to have sex. Such moves are: baring their sexual organs out completely, partially baring their sexual organs, not showing any sexual organs at all, having the clam shell open, exposing a pearl, having lost a pearl, moving, sitting, falling asleep, and having sex with another clam.

There appears to be an alpha and beta dominance that takes place between clams and their sluttiness. The alpha fucks all the betas, but the beta want to fuck the alpha, but fuck other betas while waiting to fuck the alpha. If multiple alphas exist they fuck until one alpha is the supreme alpha, who then fucks all the lesser alphas, who fuck all the betas who all have sex with each other all the time every time.

I asked him to cull this down into a workable draft of his parody article, and here's what he came back with:

Clams: The Sluts of The Ocean

The animal kingdom has left humanity with many mysteries but none more than the depths of the ocean. However, thanks to North Carolina State University's research team one such mystery, the clam, has been solved. "Clams are just crazy for clam cock," according to lead researcher David Coyne.

Indigenous to North America, Japan, Italy, and India, the hard shelled creature attained the status of "sluts drunk on clam cum" after many years of empirically observed loose morals and wanton, spread-eagled depravity. Researchers have observed a shameless display of the clam laying prostrate before any suitor. "Although many sea creatures enjoy sexual reproduction," explained researcher David Coyne, "as we observed clams reproduce, we found that there is nothing these tawdry whores won't try at least once, and probably more, because the gaping, jizz-slurping clam just can't get enough of the slutty clam-on-clam pounding it craves."

You name it clams are into it. The greater question is what doesn't turn clams on? A truck that fell off a ship, Air Supply albums, even random plans from a general contractor trying to rob a Wells Fargo—clams tried to fuck it. "I have laid witness to a clam riding another clam while trying to fuck a clam riding another clam," said Coyne, "It's common during storms as a end-of-days type fuck."

There appears to be an alpha and beta dominance that takes place between clams and their sluttiness. "The alpha fucks all the betas," explained Coyne, "but the betas want to fuck the alpha, while also wanting to fuck other betas who are waiting to fuck the alpha." Researchers explained that if multiple alphas exist they fuck until one alpha is the supreme alpha, who then fucks all the lesser alphas, who fuck all the betas who all fuck each other as much as clam possible. With all this sex it has been measured that a clam can produce half it's body weight in jizzem a day, and can swallow that amount in less than four seconds. It is estimated that 20% of a clam's slimy body is jizzem from a past sexual encounter.

Researchers did experiment in heightening the slutty clam experience and did attempt to slap the ass of a clam during sex. Researchers were curious if it was possible for a clam mid-sex to be sexing so hard that they'd kill another clam or itself by the sheer force of the tasteless slut-pounding. Amidst a nipple twisting clam sex experience the two clams reached their slut-pounding limit and exploded into each into blood, cum, and pearls. Within moments, other clams in the area immediately went to the floating blood, cum, pearl visage and fucked inside of it until exhaustion.

Note how the new headline, with a colon instead of an inactive verb, has better verisimilitude for a magazine parody piece. It's also slightly shorter, which is always good for a title.

I told him:

"The clam story definitely has the potential to be a laffer! The first 2 paragraphs are already working pretty well. After that, it loses the take and stops escalating. Can you write a few paragraphs more? You need to stay on track and escalate: you have two tracks going: the editorial voice calling out the clams as harlots, and the scientific findings about how craven and sexual they are. Need to push both—religious leaders being upset about them, causing minor sex tsunamis from all their fucking, causing clam-sex deaths in Bangladesh, etc., more extreme off-the-hook fucking scenarios involving clams—escalate on the track you established! I would ALSO like you to escalate the nonsensicalness. Because this idea is so silly, it needs to get crazy and make less sense as it proceeds.

"I tinkered with the story after reading through it. Here's as far as I got...

"The animal kingdom has left humanity with many mysteries but none more than the depths of the ocean. However, thanks to North Carolina State University's research team one such mystery, the clam, has been solved. 'Clams are just crazy for clam cock,' according to lead researcher David Coyne.

"Indigenous to North America, Japan, Italy, and India, the hard shelled creature attained the status of 'sluts drunk on clam cum' after many years of empirically observed loose morals and wanton, spread-eagled depravity. Researchers have observed a shameless display of the clam laying prostrate before any suitor. 'Although many sea creatures enjoy sexual reproduction,' Coyne says, 'as we observed clams reproduce, we found that there is nothing these tawdry sea whores won't try at least once, and probably more, because the gaping, jizz-slurping clam just can't get enough of the slutty clam-on-clam pounding it craves.'

"You name it clams are into it. The bigger question for clam-sex science is what doesn't enflame the insatiable erotic desires of the filthy, filthy, clam? A truck that fell off a ship, Air Supply albums, even random plans from a general contractor trying to rob a Wells Fargo—the the cum-breathing trollop clam tried to fuck it or get fucked by it. 'I have witnessed to a clam riding another clam while trying to fuck a clam riding another clam,' said Coyne."

He did one more draft:

Clams: The Sluts of The Ocean

The animal kingdom has left humanity with many mysteries but none more than the depths of the ocean. However, thanks to North Carolina State University's research team one such mystery, the clam, has been solved. "Clams are just crazy for clam cock," according to lead researcher David Coyne.

Indigenous to North America, Japan, Italy, and India, the hard shelled creature attained the status of "sluts drunk on clam cum" after many years of empirically observed loose morals and wanton, spread-eagled depravity. Researchers have observed a shameless display of the clam laying prostrate before any suitor. "Although many sea creatures enjoy sexual reproduction,"

Coyne says, "as we observed clams reproduce, we found that there is nothing these tawdry sea whores won't try at least once, and probably more, because the gaping, jizz-slurping clam just can't get enough of the slutty clam-on-clam pounding it craves."

You name it clams are into it. The bigger question for clam-sex science is what doesn't inflame the insatiable erotic desires of the filthy, filthy, clam? A truck that fell off a ship, Air Supply albums, even random plans from a general contractor trying to rob a Wells Fargo—the the cum-breathing trollop clam tried to fuck it or get fucked by it. "I have witnessed a clam riding another clam while trying to fuck a clam riding another clam," said Coyne.

The effects of so much clam-based fucking has caused worldly effects. "We're calling them 'sex-tsunamis,'" said Coyne, "the shear force generated from the perpetual pounding of a gaudy clam fuck orgy is enough to topple boats." The coast of Northern Florida is reeling the most from the sleazy slut-bag clams. Waves have been reported to reach up to a 14 foot face, and surfers have become uninterested shortly after science defined the phenomenon as "giant waves of cum." With a clam able to produce twice it's body weight in cum a day, and swallow it in under four seconds scientists fear the "sex-tsunamis" could become more and more powerful. "If all the clams came together and then came together," paused Coyne, "the whole eastern seaboard would be at risk from one big tidal-cum-wave."

With world ending potential religious zealots have begun to weigh in. "This sleazy display of smut from such creatures will not be our end. The Holy Trinity won't allow it," exclaimed the Vatican. However confident the Vatican did concede that The Father, The Son, and The Holy Spirit never quite fucked like one of these hoeing clams. The Bible does cover many apocalyptic scenarios but clam cum isn't one of them. Many believe the end is nigh because of these dick munching clams and are coming together to wait for the end. Others however, are following in the clam's slutty-steps by coming together and waiting for the end by cumming together.

I made a few tweaks and purchased the article for *Blaffo*.

CHAPTER 14 ACTION STEP

Seek out short comedy you like. It can be sketch, prose, or any kind of format. Analyze it. See how the core funny idea is introduced and then escalated with narrow precision and joke discipline. See what Funny Filters are at work. See how it conforms to the best practices outlined in this book.

15

COMMON MISTAKES

I've seen thousands of short comedy pieces written by everyone from inexperienced beginners to the best satirical writers in the world. In every case, there's something about the piece that can be improved. It's a rare piece that's anywhere close to perfect. Some pieces just need a couple of tweaks. Others need more fundamental changes. A great many need to be rewritten entirely. Some need to be scraped outright. But all need something. And if it's not just a couple of tweaks, it's probably on this list of the most common mistakes in short comedy pieces, sketches, or bits.

If you think your piece suffers from one or more of these, you're probably right. This list is presented with the most common problems first.

1. The wrong concept was chosen.

All too often, especially in beginners' work, a piece may be structured well and written competently, but it's all for naught, because the title isn't funny, the core concept is flawed, and therefore no one is ever going to read the piece. Beyond that, the piece usually isn't worth reading, because when you escalate a title joke that isn't funny, you get a longer piece of writing that doesn't usually get any funnier.

2. It's off-take.

This is one of the trickiest problems for the writer to self-diagnose. It takes a smart beta reader to know the language of criticism well enough to explain why it's the wrong take. Inexperienced beta readers will instinctively know it's the wrong take, but they won't have the words to express it. Instead, if you've trained them to be honest, they'll say things like, "I expected it to be different," "It's a funny idea, but I just didn't think the story was funny," or "It kind of went in a strange direction." If they're still stuck in the polite stage of criticism, they'll simply point out the one off-take joke in your piece that they found passably amusing.

If this happens to your piece, ask questions of your beta readers to get at the heart of what they expected from the title. Get them to explain the piece they wanted. This will give you great clues to find the right take for your concept.

3. It starts with the right take, but then veers off track.

This happens a lot. The title sets the stage and the audience is already laughing or at least primed to laugh, but then one or two joke beats in, the writer gets tired of the concept or the take and decides to move the story in a different direction. The writer thinks they're making the story more interesting, but all they're doing is abandoning the reader. They're forgetting the First Laugh. The piece has no joke discipline, and it fails.

4. It's in the wrong format or medium.

People tend to write their pieces in a trendy format, like a listicle or fake news. But these aren't always the best format choices. If a fake news story is heavy with quotes from one character, and those quotes make up most of the joke beats, that piece should probably be rewritten as a first-person essay in the voice of that character. That will allow the core joke to shine. If a piece is dialog heavy or action oriented, a sketch is usually the best choice. If you don't have the means to perform or record a sketch, even a sketch presented as a written script would be a better presentation format for an action- or dialog-heavy piece.

Consider whether street art or the stage are better media for your concept. Imagine your material in a number of different formats to see where it's funniest. If you're using a parody construct, you're best off using the same format as the thing you're parodying. For example, "George Lucas In Love," the short piece that launched director Joe Nussbaum's career, was a parody of the movie *Shakespeare In Love*, so, naturally, he produced his piece as a film.

5. It doesn't escalate.

This happens in a lot of writing, but primarily in sketches. Variations of the same joke beat are repeated without escalating stakes, tension, adding other Funny Filters, or expanding the world. An audience will quickly lose interest in a piece that doesn't escalate.

6. It's too complicated.

A piece that's too complicated often looks complicated and hard to read, with thick, dense prose, big words, and no paragraph breaks. Beyond that, the sentences will be long, it will be hard to follow, and it will possibly contain more than one impossible thing or different rules in the comedy universe that clash logically. The writer may be trying to accomplish too much, or challenge the reader, thinking that will enhance the reading experience. All this will do is make the piece unreadable. A comedy piece should be simple, almost like you're reciting the ABCs: concept, joke beat one, joke beat two, etc. It should be easy for anyone to follow, and only be about one thing.

Complicated, hard-to-read pieces are common. Writers often have the problem of getting bored with their concepts after they've sat with them for a while, and they wrongly think that simply rolling out their concept in simple, well-paced joke beats will be too boring for the reader. It's important for the writer to remember that the reader will not have sat with this concept for more than a few seconds. If it got a laugh when you first tested the title, trust that your reader also laughed when they first heard it, and trust they will stay with you if you sustain that laughter for a few additional joke beats riffing on the same concept. The far greater danger is that the piece will be too complicated.

If you're worried about your story being too simple, consider this: I've seen hundreds of stories that were too complicated. I've never seen a story that was too simple. That mistake didn't even make this list.

7. It doesn't have a title.

No one will read a block of prose with no title on it. If you came up with a funny title but simple forgot to put it atop your article, that's an easy fix. If you never wrote a title in the first place and your piece was written regardless, you can almost certainly scrap that piece. It's difficult enough to come up with funny titles when you have no parameters. Trying to come up with a funny title that perfectly fits an already-existent piece is like trying to put scrambled eggs back together. Always start with a title.

8. There's no verisimilitude.

Even experienced writers who understand the importance of verisimilitude will often fall short, revealing in subtle ways throughout their piece that it's less than a fully serious, legitimate work in the format at hand. Verisimilitude must be maintained in format, character voice, narrator voice, editorial voice, and details about your world.

When there's no verisimilitude, or not a lot, a comedy piece comes off as light fun, an amusing diversion like all other comedy. But when the verisimilitude is turned up to the hilt, magic happens. The comedy rises to a new level of quality and gets bigger, broader laughs.

There's almost no ceiling to good verisimilitude. The more you can add, the funnier your work will be. *National Lampoon* raised the bar on verisimilitude in the last century with the strikingly accurate designs they created for their parodies. *The Onion* was popular and amusing before 1995 when it looked like a goofy campus tabloid, but after 1995, when the publication was redesigned to look exactly like a real newspaper, its success rose to new heights.

The LiarTownUSA parodies never fail to elicit fits of laughter, and a big part of their appeal is verisimilitude. Good verisimilitude gets people talking and sharing material. LiarTownUSA pieces have become Internet memes. Entertainment industry professionals have approached

LiarTownUSA creator Sean Tejaratchi to offer him TV writing jobs.

9. The Subtext is stated overtly.

A piece isn't funny if you show your hand and spell out your secret message. Subtext needs to stay unsaid. In order for your piece to work, your reader needs to be allowed to add two and two and figure out the Subtext on their own.

If you reveal your Subtext, you won't know you're doing it. If your Subtext is that humans aren't kind to other animals, you're not going to say, "The meaning of this story is that humans should be kinder to animals." What you'll do is write a funny story about a zoo or puppy farm or some such, and one of the characters will say, "I mean, that's what people do, we're just fucking mean as fuck to these goats." You'll think that's a joke beat because you'll know it has the Shock Funny Filter and funny specificity working for it, but really all you're doing is revealing your Subtext, which not only fails as a joke beat, it takes your piece down with it.

10. It contains off-take jokes

Audiences love joke discipline. In many ways, this is the core skill they love to watch writers perform almost like they're watching an Olympic sporting event: how faithfully can the writer adhere to the core concept while still escalating each joke beat? If the writer can do it well, the audience will be delighted just as they would watching a figure skater perform successive flip-jumps.

FUNNIER-WRITING TIP #18: DON'T USE WACKY CHARACTER NAMES

First-time humor writers often try to give their characters silly names (names that rhyme with or sound like famous names, or names that sound crazy), or give funny titles or acronyms that spell out a funny word to organizations within their comedy world. This is okay in funny children's stories or stories that use dramatic structure (chapter 16), but it's a mistake in short comedically structured writing, whether sketch, prose, or stand-up. A silly name might get a laugh, but it's an off-take joke, a cheap laugh that comes at the expense of the more satisfying humor that comes from the verisimilitude of a realistic, unnoticeable name in a piece, or a character otherwise played straight. Names that disappear in this way and become part of the fabric of a comedy world, without calling undue attention to themselves, further the greater goal of the writer's lack of awareness that there's anything humorous afoot. The audience doesn't want you to wink or smirk or be cute for their perceived benefit. They want you to play it straight, and stay on track.

Sometimes off-take jokes happen when the writer isn't confident in the concept. They'll throw in audience-pleasing distractions like a wacky name for a character, a funny acronym of the organization they represent, wacky dialog, or screaming dialog (which is almost never funny in prose). All of these things indicate that your story is sinking. This is what happens when a writer fails to stick with the take promised by the title, or finds their take isn't bringing forth an adequate bounty of jokes, so in desperation they turn to these easy, off-take jokes to get laughs. These jokes destroy verisimilitude and repel readers, telling them they're in the hands of a writer who doesn't know how to control or manipulate an audience. They'd no sooner trust a carny who has no control over a roller coaster.

11. It doesn't have enough well-paced joke beats.

Sometimes a whole paragraph will go by without a joke beat. This usually means the piece has died. Luckily, you can resuscitate a piece like like as long as the title, take, and remainder of the piece are good. Just add more joke beats. You want a joke beat at least every couple of lines in prose, and at least every few seconds in a stand-up bit or sketch.

12. It has clichés.

Relying on clichés for joke beats within a story is a rookie mistake. Some clichés will still get laughs from some audiences, but since they'll turn off the tastemakers and sophisticates, they're best avoided if you want the greatest chance of success.

13. It doesn't make sense.

Sometimes a title is selected that no one gets, or just doesn't make any sense. Usually, this happens when no feedback group was employed and the title was never tested. If the title doesn't make sense, the piece won't be read. If a title is funny but the story doesn't make sense, readers may trust it for a line or two based on the title, but as soon as they realize it doesn't make sense, they'll give up on it. Readers want to be controlled and led down a path. Don't make them do any work figuring out what you're saying. Lay the path out clearly, and leave as little as possible up to their interpretation.

14. It's sloppy or lazy.

A comma in the wrong place or the lack of a hyphen in a compound adjective may seem like tiny problems, but such oversights can confuse the meaning in a phrase, and therefore ruin a joke beat and possibly derail a readers' enjoyment enough for them to give up on the piece. Proof your work. There's no excuse not to.

Another indication of a lazy piece of writing is a piece that's too short. A story should only be as long as it has to be, but if you have a funny title, you can almost always write at least 200-500 words to go with it. If, on the other hand, your piece is a parody of something short, by all means write it short. But if you're parodying, say, a *National Geographic* travel piece, writing a hundred words or less tells the audience you didn't care enough to give them more joke beats, and they'll give up on you.

CHAPTER 15 ACTION STEP

Go through your piece and make sure it's not making any of these 14 mistakes. If it is, correct them.

DON'T BE SO DRAMATIC

It's a good idea to become proficient at the fundamental skill of writing a joke before you delve into writing a longer piece of comedy like a short half-page piece. And it's a good idea to become proficient at writing a short piece before writing something as advanced as a comedy screenplay, sitcom, or comic novel. So many writers want to jump right into writing these extremely complicated forms when they're barely familiar with simpler forms, and it's almost always a mistake.

When you're ready to try something funny that's longer, here is what you need to know:

If you want to write anything longer than a line or two, a short scene, more than a page or two of prose, or a few pages of a script, you're in an entirely different universe of structure. Comedic structure will fall apart if you try to sustain it any longer. Instead of comedic structure, you need to use traditional dramatic structure. That's what's required to hold an audience's interest beyond the roughly five minutes allotted by comedic structure. If you attempt to string out comedic structure any longer, you'll only succeed in creating what feels like a painfully long comedy sketch that won't end.

Conversely, dramatically structured writing isn't limited to longer-form work. You can write funny drama as short as you want. Traditional word-of-mouth jokes use dramatic structure (like, "A rabbi, a priest and a monk walk into a bar"). Simon Rich plays with dramatic structure in some of his extremely short pieces as well.

FUNNIER-WRITING TIP #19: EVERY WORD MATTERS

In writing a one-line joke, you learned to omit needless words. That task continues in the writing of a longer piece, whether structured comedically or dramatically. You might write needless words in your story without giving it a second thought. You're just trying to fill out space, right? Wrong. By all means, fill space and write needless words in your rough draft, but when you're completing your final draft, every word must be needed. Every word must be either setting up a joke, delivering a joke, providing vital exposition, or moving the story forward. And it must do so economically. Timing is one of the most important tools of comedy. If you're rambling and not choosing every word carefully, you're squandering what little chance you have to control the timing of your work.

According to master of story Joseph Campbell, we're all born with an innate understanding—even need—for story structure. It's how we make sense of our existence. We use story as an analogy for our lives, one that helps us face moral questions, psychic struggles, and existential crises. Story is the lifeblood of all religions. According to famed psychiatrist Carl Jung, our need for story is revealed in our dreams. It's something hardwired into our brains.

We may all have an innate understanding of story, but mastering the telling of stories is a learned skill that, like any, takes practice.

This chapter is a top-level overview of story structure. I encourage you to make a study of dramatic structure beyond this book, especially if you're embarking on a comedy screenplay. There are so many great books about story structure, and it's a long journey to master it.

As you write a comedic story using dramatic structure, most of the feedback you get will be based more on the dramatic structure than on the comedy or any jokes. People will tell you "I didn't believe this character would do that," or "I lost interest at about page 30—nothing seemed to be happening." Another typical problem with comedy screenplays is that the comedy will likely bleed too much into your dramatic structure, leaving your audience unable to invest any emotion in the story, which they must in order to be pulled into it. Mostly, your dramatic structure just won't be strong enough, therefore your comedy won't work as well as it should. Dramatically structured works of comedy need a strong dramatic foundation. Only then can the comedy work.

All drama requires three basic things that are fundamentally different from (and not part of) comedic structure:

1. Characters we care about. This doesn't mean we have to like them. We just have to have empathy for them. We have to be interested in what happens to them, ideally on an emotional level. This is much different from comedic structure, where characters are two-dimensional and we're only meant to laugh at them. There are a few things that make us care about a character, but none is more powerful than giving that character an obsessive passion to achieve their goal. In any story, the audience is naturally drawn to the character for whom they have the most empathy, and who will stop at nothing to achieve a goal despite enormous obstacles.

2. Unanswered questions. Good storytellers lead us into a story, seducing us by making us ask questions and wonder what will happen next. Once we care about a character, a storyteller dangles two possibilities before us at all times: will something good happen to the character(s) or something bad? The open question, minute to minute, of whether a wonderful outcome or terrible outcome will occur, pulls an audience into a story. It works best when this deepening question concerns characters' relationships with other characters in the story, when there's more

at stake. But more intellectual or plot-based questions can also be asked. *The Matrix* is a great example of a movie that poses continual and deepening questions about what's going on. Even the tag line for the movie was a question: "What is the Matrix?" The filmmakers teased the audience by only giving them a trickle of answers as the film went on, whetting our appetite for more information, all the while introducing more, deeper questions.

3. Resolution. This is the whole point of story. This is what makes art different from life. Your protagonist or some other character in your story must learn something or change as a result of the story. There needs to be a reason the story was told. Loose ends, for the most part, need to be tied up. All the questions asked in the story need to be answered.

ADDING COMEDIC MOMENTS TO DRAMATIC WRITING

Before delving deeper into dramatic structure, let's tackle the relatively simple task of writing comedic moments within a serious dramatic work. You already know how to do this from everything you've read here and in *How to Write Funny*, but let's look at how that applies.

In a serious dramatic story, funny moments that lighten up the mood are sometimes necessary to let the audience catch their breath, enjoy some literal comic relief amid a lot of heavy, dark, or sad drama. You have 11 tools to do that. The Funny Filters can be combined in any number of ways to devise an almost infinite variety of funny sequences to provide the levity you need.

Working within a more serious drama actually makes the job of writing comedy easier, because the drama serves as a built-in straight voice, and therefore you get automatic contrast, tension that the audience is eager to see relieved. Also, Subtext is usually at the ready, arising naturally from the theme of the story or central drive of a scene. Playing off the seriousness, throwing in a few lines crafted like jokes using the Funny Filers, will give the audience permission to laugh, and they'll be grateful for the opportunity. The Funny Filters that work especially well against a backdrop of serious drama are Character, Irony, Madcap, Metahumor, and Shock. Here are some examples of other Funny Filters used in dramatic movies:

In *E.T.*, when the kids' mother looks in the closet, where we're sure she'll find E.T., go berserk, and perhaps alert the authorities, the camera pans across a pile of stuffed animal faces looking back at her, E.T.'s among them, unmoving as if he's one of the stuffed animals. This great comedic moment uses Character-Irony (putting E.T. in a context where he's insignificant and lifeless when we know he's important and full of life) and Misplaced Focus, the camera literally focusing on the entirety of the stuffed animals as opposed to E.T.

In *Hidden Figures*, when the women's car breaks down, one of them makes a Reference joke about her co-worker "sitting in the back of the bus." Irony on top of Irony is used when an officer pulls them over and is surprised to learn they work for NASA, but then offers to escort them to work. Metahumor is added on top when the women acknowledge the Irony and laugh about it.

In *Mask*, comedic moments are used repeatedly to release tension and define characters. A simple but effective Wordplay (word repetition) callback joke is used when Rocky, the boy with the rare bone disorder, is introduced to his class on the first day of school. Another new student is introduced first, she waves, and the other students applaud and cheer her. Flattered, she says, "Wow! Thanks a lot." When Rocky is introduced, he waves to the class, but the other students don't applaud or cheer. Rocky lowers his hand and, after a pregnant pause, jokes, "Wow. Thanks a lot." A good number of kids get a laugh out of the line, and the teacher winks at him.

In *Castaway*, Tom Hanks' character creates fire after a long, frustrating struggle. When he succeeds, he combines Reference (singing the Doors song "Light My Fire") and the Character archetype of the Man-Child, free-associating like a happy kid, reacting to the situation with an abundance of playful emotion. He shouts like a caveman, "I have made fire!" playing a caveman character and parodying tropes of caveman stories.

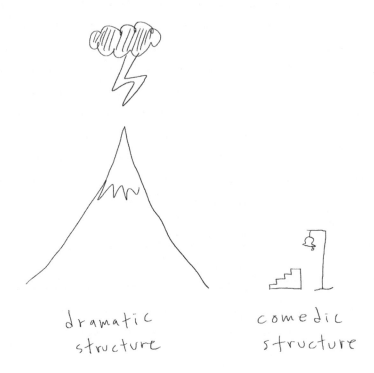

dramatic
structure

comedic
structure

Most of these clips can be found online. The same simple techniques can be used in novels, stage plays, and any other longer form.

Another way to introduce comedy in a dramatic work is to reduce dramatic characters to simple character archetypes within a scene. Another is to introduce an entirely new comic-relief character. It may be a character featured in only one scene, like The Larry Miller suck-up store manager in *Pretty Woman*. Or it can be a minor character who pops up at key moments, like Bill Murray's famously uncredited roll in *Tootsie*. These characters are almost always archetypes.

In a single short scene that furthers the dramatic story, comedic structure can be used to make a funny scene in an otherwise serious or dramatic film, escalating a comedic concept unique to the scene, and then capping it off with a button. This works only when the scene fulfills the larger purpose of furthering the dramatic action.

There's a scene in *The Shawshank Redemption* that uses comedic structure. When Andy and his friends are sorting books for the new prison library, Heywood reads off titles for books and pronounces them wrong. This is the joke track of the scene. It escalates beautifully, first with Heywood having slight difficulty reading a longer name (Robert Louis Stevenson), then in the next beat mispronouncing *The Count of Monte Cristo* as "Crisco," escalating the Wordplay. One of the other inmates laughs at him, escalating the tension. In the next beat, he mispronounces the book's author, Alexandre Dumas, as "dumb ass," escalating the Wordplay more by introducing Shock. When Andy explains that the book is about a prison break, the character of Red provides the button for the scene, suggesting they put the book in the "educational" section of the library.

DRAMATIC STRUCTURE

In his seminal book, *Poetics*, Aristotle broke down drama into three essential types, all of which use the three basic ingredients above, but each in unique ways. These three types still define the parameters of what drama is to this day:

1. Unity of Time

Unity of Time uses either contiguous time or a central temporal event as the structural nexus of a story. This works best on stage, since the action there is in reality locked within a certain time period, whereas in other media time can be played with. Examples of this kind of structure: *Home for the Holidays*, directed by Jodie Foster, where the story is structured around a Thanksgiving gathering. This structure can come off feeling arty, experimental, and somewhat untethered unless it's done at the highest skill level. However, if done well, its effect can be powerful. It can stir up deep feelings within the audience, like our pull toward cultural traditions or major life passages that touch us on an instinctive level. It does this in a way that other dramatic structures can't. *Slacker* and *Ameri-*

can Graffiti are two other movies that use the Unity of Time structure for comedy.

2. Unity of Place

Unity of Place is similar to Unity of Time in terms of its powerful effect. Using a place as the central focus of the structure creates a feeling of nostalgia, which is difficult to achieve in traditionally structured comedy or drama. Unity of Place dramas aren't as rare as Unity of Time dramas, but they're still rare. Robert Altman often made Unity of Place movies. Unity of place comedies generate laughs by collecting strange or funny characters in the place, or by featuring a series of unrelated vignettes that showcase the place. Walt Disney's Oscar-winning short, *The Old Mill,* shows all the various life and animal families around an old windmill. *Cinema Paradiso* is a series of semi-related vignettes centered around an old cinema. Typically in a Unity of Place drama the place is also the title of the work.

One of the early acts of *The Right Stuff* uses this structure effectively, focusing on Pancho's Bar near Edwards Air Force Base. *American Graffiti* uses both Unity of Time and Unity of Place structure. (The time is Curt's last night in his hometown as well as the end of his youth, and the place is the hometown, more specifically "the strip.") It's not surprising that *American Graffiti* is the product of one of the modern geniuses of story structure, George Lucas. It's also not surprising that the 1973 film remains the fourth highest grossing teen comedy of all time. It's a powerful story, tapping deeper into the American psyche than most movies can ever hope to with their run-of-the-mill, traditional, or "Unity of Action" structure.

3. Unity of Action

This is the structure used in 99.99 percent of all the drama or long-form comedy that we see today, in any medium. This is where action leads to other action, propelling the story forward through cause and effect. When people say "traditional story structure," this is what they're talking about. There are many genres within this structure, like the epic myth, the fairytale, the love story, and others, and there are still more subgenres within each genre. Going into those in any depth is beyond the scope of this book. Suffice it to say, most genres within the Unity of Action structure all follow some variation of the epic myth structure, popularly known as the "hero's journey." Most of the humorous short stories, novels, TV shows, and movies you see abide by a watered-down version of this structure. So let's look at what that structure is. It features the following steps, often in this order but not necessarily.

THE ORDINARY WORLD

This shows the protagonist(s) in their regular world, before any adventure begins. This is Jim Carrey in the first act of *Liar Liar* blissfully going though his life lying to everyone he knows, playing the sleazy lawyer who will say anything to make money, establishing him as a character we love to hate. This stage of a story also hints at the protagonist's inner need—a flaw this story will force them to face and probably correct.

INCITING INCIDENT

A wrench is thrown into the protagonist/hero's life, and their life will never be the same again. The dramatic question (or hook) is, how will they deal with it? This is when Arthur Dent's house is demolished by an interstellar superhighway in *The Hitchhiker's Guide to the Galaxy*. This situation calls the hero to either act or react in a meaningful way.

REFUSAL / LOCK-IN

This is when the hero denies the action or impending journey. Joseph Campbell calls this "refusal of the call." This heightens the contrast and increases the dramatic conflict, creating more of an emotional roller-coaster ride for the audience. This is when Bill (Keanu Reeves) in *Bill and Ted's Excellent Adventure* says, "No way!" in response to the call by his future self to go on an adventure through history. Lock-in happens after a motivating event. When future Bill and Ted accurately guess the number present-day Bill and Ted are thinking of (69), this blows their minds and they're convinced and motivated to go on the adventure—just try to stop them. They are locked in.

TRAINING / GATHERING ALLIES / MEETING MENTOR

Once the hero of the story enters the new world introduced in the inciting incident, there may be training necessary for them to succeed at whatever is required. Most importantly, and most typically in comedies, there are allies to gather. These are all the new people your protagonist meets in the new world who will help the hero (and the audience) navigate the new world. It's when Marlin meets Dory and the other creatures of the ocean, like the sharks and the turtles, in *Finding Nemo*. We'll also, of course, meet people who will resist the hero and their friends. These are the antagonist and the antagonist's minions. Some allies may appear to be good but end up betraying the hero, which always makes for an exciting dramatic reversal in a story.

RISING TENSION / RISING STAKES

There's more at stake now. So, worse things will happen if the hero fails. Maybe comrades will be hurt if they don't succeed. This is usually several scenes or sequences of ever-increasing tension in a story. An example is when Ferris Bueller is in danger of getting himself and his friends caught playing hooky by a sniveling Chicago waiter. The waiter is one in a series of "threshold guardians" in that excellently structured story. The hero and the audience get deeper into the story. They try to solve their problem as they embark on their mission, but sometimes they make it worse, heightening the dramatic tension.

TESTS / FALSE DEFEAT / VICTORY

The hero has either appeared to win or appeared to lose, and the central mission appears to be in jeopardy. This usually happens roughly midway through a story. The middle of the story is made up of several tests or confrontations with various threshold guardians whom the hero sometimes defeats, sometimes is harmed by, but ultimately strengthened by. With each new advance, the hero is more prepared to meet the ultimate challenge than before. This is when Bill Murray confronts a possessed Sigourney Weaver in *Ghostbusters*.

ALL IS LOST

This is when it seems the hero has lost and there's no way to succeed. This is often a "visit with death" moment. In many longer stories, the hero or someone close to the hero actually dies. In comedies, it's often a symbolic death, a threat of death, or the death of the soul or an idea. In *Ferris Bueller's Day Off*, Cameron fake-drowns in the pool and genuinely frightens Ferris. In *The Blues Brothers*, it's Jake Blues' wife threatening to kill the Blues Brothers, firing her machine gun repeatedly at them at close range. In *Anchorman: The Legend of Ron Burgundy*, Ron Burgundy lets himself go and becomes a bum after he believes his career is over. In that case, his career has died.

ORDEAL / NEW TWIST

The protagonist summons a deeper, inner strength, wisdom, or ally they gained from the adventure, and uses it to summon one last desperate chance at snatching victory from the jaws of defeat. In *Home Alone*, this is when the scary old man who lives next door bursts in and knocks out the crooks with a shovel. Kevin is saved by his earlier befriending of this neighbor. The adventure taught Kevin the old man wasn't scary at all—he was actually nice.

RESOLUTION / REWARD

Now, the hero wins the day, defeats their foe, internal or external, and by doing so solves their inner need and/or outer goal as well as saving themselves and/or others. The hero makes a transformation, either in themselves or in the lives of others. In ancient storytelling, this was the hero gaining an elixir from the gods to give to the people that will save them. In *The 40-Year-Old Virgin*, this is when Andy finally admits to Trish that he's a virgin and they get married.

DENOUEMENT

Many longer stories have this final step. This is when our hero enjoys their victory after having succeeded in their journey. It's also where the hero actually delivers the elixir to the people. In *Trading Places*, this is when they're on the beach, drinking mai tais.

There are other, smaller steps you can find in dramatic structure and add to your work if you care to investigate the subject further. There's also different emphasis on different steps depending on the genre of the story. A story in the action genre will emphasize training, for example. In comedy, allies and mentors and opponents are often stressed, because most of the comedy springs from the relationships between the characters.

There are also some exceptions to the steps above, sometimes depending on genre, sometimes depending on the length of the story. The shorter the story, the fewer minor steps it needs. Inciting incident, rising tension, and resolution are the minimum requirements for any story.

For the most part, just about any story you tell that's comedic, but longer than five minutes, is going to need to abide by something very close to this structure. It's a rule, of course, not a law, so it can be bent and often is. But veer from it at your peril. It works because it's time-tested. And it's always best to experiment with shorter work before trying to tackle longer work.

Check out David Sedaris's stories to see dramatic structure in action in shorter-form work. To see it in longer form, read any comic novel or watch any comedy movie and analyze the structure. No matter how silly or "non-dramatic" you might think it is, you'll see it following this structure. The only comedy movies that don't follow this structure are sketch movies, which use comedic structure in each of the sketches, then string those sketches through a framing device. And usually this framing device, no matter how brief, employs dramatic structure. "Weird Al" Yankovic's *UHF* is an example.

SITCOM WRITING

TV sitcoms use dramatic structure as well, but in this shorter format it doesn't have to be as epic a structure as a novel, movie, or stage play. Here everything is toned down.

A sitcom will still have the basic elements of an inciting incident, rising tension, and resolution, but it won't present a whole new world for the protagonist. Often it will only be a small misunderstanding, an itch that needs to be scratched, or a budding obsession that needs to be checked.

TV is a strange medium when it comes to story, because resolution isn't the goal. The goal on TV is to get the audience to keep watching through the commercials. So, the medium takes advantage of the human need for dramatic resolution, and keeps audiences engaged in a story with continual unanswered questions served up before the commercial breaks, or stringing them along as cliffhangers between episodes. On Netflix, which doesn't have commercials but which is run by people who nonetheless want you to keep watching, the answers to dramatic questions are left unanswered at the end of each episode. Audiences can't stop watching, and they binge. There's rarely resolution on TV.

SUBPLOTS

Movies and novels often have subplots, plots that also use dramatic structure but that are secondary to the main plot and usually interwoven at the climax. Subplots allow the writer to explore the theme of a story from a different angle.

TV has evolved to require a more robust subplot system. To keep the stories on sitcoms more interesting to as many viewers as possible, writers of sitcoms create as many as three stories and weave them together. The A story is the main story, where most of the action and time is focused. The B and C stories are smaller, largely unrelated to the A story except possibly the involvement of the same characters. They nonetheless provide variations on a theme. Smaller even than the C story is a "runner," which is a succession of escalating joke beats that's strung through an episode of a sitcom. It usually involves no more than three or four beats culminating with a button. It's like a mini-sketch within a shhow.

COMEDIC CONCEPTS

What makes a larger work funny as opposed to serious or dramatic? You need only look to the Funny Filters. If the concept employs one or more of the Funny Filters, the story can be told comedically. If the main character is the opposite type of character required for the journey, you have Irony, and you would emphasize the opposing forces to create dramatic conflict. If a comedic archetype is the star, you can use the Character Funny Filter to show that character acting on their traits and getting into deeper trouble and confronting rising stakes. Usually, Character and

Irony will both be present: *Inner Space, Liar Liar, Finding Nemo,* and *Galaxy Quest* are good examples of movies best executed as comedies because of their ironic concepts.

Here's an example of a short comedy piece written using dramatic story structure. It was written by Miles Falkenstein and published in *Blaffo.*

Tom Hanks Had Sex with My Wife and I Am Fine with It

Have you ever wondered if the life you know is crumbling apart? Have you ever felt like the passion you felt is no longer there? I certainly have.

My name is Mark Richardson. My wife Stacy and I had been married for 5 years and, to be honest, things had not been going well. We had been growing apart and just didn't have that same spark. She was even saying she didn't want children anymore. Really the only moments we enjoyed together was watching Tom Hanks movies.

I was worried the marriage was doomed unless something drastic happened. You could say I was waiting for a miracle.

One evening after a particularly hard day at work, I drove up to my home and noticed a tall handsome man walking out of the front door holding a bag. As I pulled in the driveway I was stunned to see that it was Tom Hanks taking out the trash at my house! I immediately jumped out of the car and ran up to shake his hand.

"Oh my god. Oh my sweet god! I am such a huge fan!" I exclaimed. "Thank you!" Tom replied. "Why are you at my house?" I asked, in shock. "Oh, Ha! Right. This must be very confusing. I was just having sex with your wife, Stacy." Tom said, smiling warmly.

I was taken back. I couldn't believe what I was hearing. I ran as fast as I could into my house. Through the front door, past the living room, and into our bedroom...

There she was, too exhausted to speak, hair completely tousled, body covered in sweat, and clutching a cigarette in her right hand. Odd, considering she had never smoked before in her life. I could tell by looking at her that this was the happiest she had ever been. I asked "Did you just get woodied by fucking Tom Hanks?" She reached for her phone and texted "yes" in her notes and showed me. I fell to my knees. With tears in my eyes. My voice shaking, I said to her "Stacy, that is single-handedly, by far, the most fucking cool thing that has ever happened to me."

At that moment Tom walked in the bedroom, picked me up off the floor, and gave me the warmest hug I've ever felt. "Thank you. Thank you so much Tom Hanks." I said into his ear, tears gushing onto his collared shirt. "How about I go get some pizza and a few beers and we'll watch the Chargers game?" Tom proposed. "Yes" my wife and I replied, simultaneously. This was the moment I knew Tom Hanks was my new best friend. My only friend, really.

Stacy and I got our spark back. All thanks to Tom Hanks' gump-fucking my wife better than she'd ever experienced previously. After thanking him, I watched as Tom said to me sincerely that he'd be glad to do it for me anytime. Not wanting to miss a good opportunity, I said "How does twice a week sound?" Tom was thrilled with my offer. He even said I could watch.

Stacy had also decided that she wanted children after all. She said that Hanks DNA being on the table changed everything. Or in her words, "The man's spunk is gold."

And you know, my friends think I'm getting shit on. Calling me "Cuck Richardson." But the truth is they can fuck off cuz Tom Hanks fucked my wife so goddamn good that it has turned my crumbling marriage around and changed my life for the better. Tom Hanks, award winning Hollywood actor, plowed my wife so exquisitely that she has decided not to leave me after all. I owe my happiness to that man and will be honored to raise his offspring.

We are naming the child Tom Hanks 2.

Notice how this story has a vaguely sympathetic character, dramatic hooks and questions, rising tension and resolution. It also has an inciting incident ("One evening . . ."), resolution (Stacy decides she wants children after all), and a denouement, which ends the story with a nice little button.

The scope of this book is the short comedy piece. I've only touched on the challenges of longer works of comedy in this chapter. I'm working on a book dedicated solely to screenplays and TV pilot scripts that will go into much more detail about my method for structuring comedic movies and shows.

It's worth repeating: it's best start with short comedy and work your way up to longer work. If you think you've done that work and are ready, I recommend the following resources for a deeper dive into longer form work:

> *Story* by Robert McKee
>
> *500 Ways to Beat the Hollywood Script-writer* by Jennifer Lerch
>
> *Save the Cat* by Blake Snyder
>
> Dan Harmon's online writing about story structure for TV
>
> Wordplayer.com

CHAPTER 16 ACTION STEP

If you've written a dramatically structured piece (a short story, TV pilot, novel, or screenplay), compare it to the basic structure laid out in this chapter. Rework it to make sure it's taking the right dramatic steps.

HELLO WORLD

The first step to expanding your comedy writing horizons beyond yourself is to show your work to peers. As we've discussed, this helps you hone your voice, learn what ideas will resonate with people, and get comfortable presenting your work to others without fear or anxiety. But perhaps most importantly, it makes your writing significantly funnier.

The next step to expanding your comedy writing horizons beyond yourself is presenting your work to real audiences. The bigger the audience, the better. People who don't know you, have no preconceived notions about you, and don't care whether you succeed are the most objective barometer for the quality of your comedy. Only by testing your work with them can you grow into a skilled professional.

At first you may feel scared to show your work to strangers. It will certainly be scary to try out your jokes on a stage at an open-mic night. But your comedy writing will go nowhere unless you throw your work out into the world in any medium and see if it can fly.

If you don't feel like you're ready, by all means spend more time writing jokes, short pieces, sketches, or routines by yourself and not showing them to the public. Show them to your feedback group for review and try to learn and improve. But doing this too long will stunt your growth as a funny writer.

You'll know you're ready for real public exposure either when you feel ready or when your peers tell you consistently that your work is funny, original, and deserving of a wider audience. Regardless, you're well served releasing as much of your work into the world as soon as possible whether you think you're ready or not. Flooding the market with your work can do no harm. You might be self-conscious about it at first, but the more you put out, the less self-conscious you'll be. At worst, no one will react, and this will tell you you need to change course and improve. At best, you'll find opportunities when people who serve as threshold guardians to greater exposure may notice your work and like it.

There are two primary ways to get your work seen by real audiences and eventually get paid for it. The first is to submit your work to existing comedy brands.

SUBMITTING TO PUBLICATIONS

Look up your favorite comedy publications and see if they're accepting submissions. If they are, they likely have submission guidelines available. If they aren't, or if you can't find their guidelines, send a short email requesting them. If you get them, send material according to the guidelines. If you don't get them, send another short email giving them some idea of your qualifications to write humor. Include 10 funny titles that you believe fit their publication. Don't send completed pieces unless they ask for that. If you don't hear back, they're not interested. Try again later with new ideas after you've continued to get better. If you persist, you might one day get some feedback on your ideas, which will be extremely valuable—be sure to thank them. If they ask to see a piece or two based on your title ideas, write those and submit them.

Some online publications you can submit to right away are *Robot Butt*, *Funny Times*, *The Hard Times*, *Blaffo*, *McSweeney's*, *Omnarchy*, the *Big Jewel*, *The Belladonna*, *Weekly Humorist*, *Slackjaw*, *Little Old Lady Comedy*, and *College Humor*. There are many others. Some of them pay a small stipend. Others are non-paying but nonetheless good entry-level publications for a new writer. Are there any small comedy blogs or websites you like? Target them.

Avoid bigger publications at first. You may get lucky and get your submission noticed, but the competition is stiff, and you may be spinning your wheels. Get published in a few smaller publications beforehand so you can include links to your previously published work in your query email to major magazine editors. You'll have more luck getting paid work if you're already an experienced, published writer.

A few bigger publications to target are *Mad*, *Cracked*, *National Lampoon*, *The American Bystander*, *Playboy*, *Vanity Fair*, *Esquire*, *The New Yorker*, *Reductress*, *The Onion*, and *Reader's Digest*. Many of these publications don't accept unsolicited submissions. You can check their websites for information.

An exhaustive source on which magazines pay writers, and how much, is at whopayswriters.com. You can also check for comedy job opportunities and make use of other resources at thecomedycrowd.com.

To find the right editors to send material to, find humor stories in publications and track down the author on social media or on their website. Contact them and ask who their editor was.

When you're ready to submit to a bigger publication, submit about five title ideas along with very short (two-three sentence) descriptions of the piece that would accompany each title. Give a sense of the take.

Don't try to make your query letter funny. The comedy should be in your titles and your descriptions. Be brief, pleasant, and professional.

A large number of submissions received by editors at humor publications, both large and small, are rejected out of hand for being unsuited for their particular voice. Be sure you're familiar with the voice and humor style of the publication, and send only ideas that you believe are appropriate for them.

Some publications have similar voices, so it's possible you'll have material to send to several different publications concurrently. It's bad practice to do this. Come up with ideas unique to each publication so you never have to send out duplicate submissions. You don't want to cause a headache for an editor by making them wonder if your piece might be published somewhere else.

FUNNIER-WRITING TIP #20: CONTROL YOUR AUDIENCE

Your audience wants you to manipulate them. By delving into your writing, no matter what the medium, they're asking you to take them on a ride. Whether your ride is a short jaunt through a wacky comedy world or an emotional roller coaster through an epic comedy opera, your audience wants to hand over their brain to you and allow you to play with it. They're counting on you to take them to the edge of fear and discomfort, then release them into laughter and joy. They want to know they're in good hands. They want to know they'll be surprised and delighted and grateful for the experience. If they see any subliminal clues that you might not be adept at giving them an amazing experience (like a mediocre title or a bad first few lines that don't meet their expectations), they won't trust you, and they won't submit to the ride.

One trick to make your list of title submissions more persuasive is to include a couple of timely titles, either seasonal, holiday based, or current-events based. This will not only peak their interest (almost all publications realize timely pieces get more eyeballs than evergreen pieces), it will also show them you can think on your feet and work fast.

If an editor asks you to submit a piece, send your submission in the body of your email. Don't attach a word document or anything else.

Sometimes emails with attachments get flagged as spam; there's no point putting up an unnecessary barrier. Make it easy for an editor to see and assess your work. Make it easy and pleasant for them to deal with you.

Don't copyright your work before you send it. This is overkill and will make you look like an amateur. Professionals aren't so precious with a small piece. They trust other professionals aren't going to steal their work.

Don't ever send your resume. No one cares where you went to college or what kind of volunteer work you do. All they care is that you produce funny material.

With any submission, be respectful of the editor's time. Make sure the editor knows you'll be easy to work with. Common industry advice for these interactions is "don't be a dick." But that's a low bar. It's best to go the extra mile. Be delightful. Be fun, friendly, hard working, persistent, eager to please, cool, and nice. Never be weird, desperate, clingy, long-winded, rude, passive-aggressive, or mean.

SUBMITTING TO A COMEDIAN

You can also submit material to a stand-up comic. Most stand-up comics nowadays write their own material, but if a comedian's career is booming, they may consider taking on a writer. Write a page or two of stand-up material for a comedian you like. You can approach any comedian, but if they're not very well known or successful, they probably can't afford a writer. If they're already famous, it may be difficult to get through their phalanx of handlers. The best targets are comedians who are up and coming, who are starting to get more famous, with small TV appearances, paid tours, and growing social-media followings. They're making more money and are getting too busy to write new material, so they're uniquely poised to be open to some writing help.

If the comedian has an agent or manager, that person is usually listed on their website. Contact them with a page or two of jokes in the comedian's style expressing your interest in writing jokes for them.

You can negotiate whatever you feel is a fair rate for the material. It will depend greatly on how well known the comedian is. In general, this will pay better than publications.

SUBMITTING TO TV

You can submit to TV shows when they announce open calls for writers. You can also apply to NBC's Late Night Writer's Workshop or any number of similar programs at festivals, schools, or contests.

Competition will be fierce for any TV writing opportunities. If you haven't published any prose pieces yet, and if you haven't done much work in comedy, it's almost certainly a waste of your time to pursue a TV writing job. Comedy is a craft, and you have to learn it and get good at it before getting the top comedy jobs.

Yet another myth perpetuated by pop culture is the Willy Wonka myth: that an obscure, inexperienced writer will be "discovered" by show business and offered a once-in-a-lifetime golden ticket to a high-paying writing job in TV. The real-life stories from chapter one of this book about Simon Rich and *The Onion* may seem like this kind of rags-to-riches myth, but they're not. Simon Rich was the editor of *The Harvard Lampoon* when he got his opportunity. *The Onion* had been publishing weekly for nearly 10 years.

When you're ready for a TV job, you'll know it. You'll have built your own brand, and you'll have an agent representing you.

HOW TO GET AN AGENT

First of all, you don't need an agent. Not yet. After you sell some work and have a fighting chance to get jobs in TV or movies, then you'll need an agent. You don't need an agent for magazine submissions.

An agent is also necessary to sell a book to a traditional publisher, but nowadays having a platform is just as necessary. You get a platform by building your own brand.

An agent's job is to find you work doing comedy for other brands, but the best way to get an agent is to build your own comedy brand. When you reach a certain level of notoriety with your unique brand of comedy, agents will be eager to represent you because you're a proven self-starter who knows how to entertain people and possibly even has some experience getting paid work.

Another way to get an agent is to get a job offer in the industry. If you win a script-writing contest or get approached to be a staff writer for a TV show through a friend or colleague, agents will be eager to represent you.

To get an agent without any notoriety or accomplishments, you just need to be good at writing comedy. Getting an agent is much more difficult in this case, but not impossible. To successfully land an agent under these circumstances, you'll need to make yourself an attractive potential client. An attractive client is someone who is savvy, prolific, and serious about a career in comedy. If you've only produced a few good ideas and don't have a backlog or a savings account full of ideas at the ready, you're not an attractive candidate for an agent. But if you produce a ton of work (jokes, stories, or sketches), an agent will know you can handle the demands of a professional comedy writing job. They'll be reasonably assured you won't embarrass them if they propose you for an open slot on the staff of a TV show.

A minimum level of social skill is required to work with an agent. A lot of people in comedy are strange. Some lack social skills. If the agent perceives you as a genius and finds your lack of social skills endearing, no problem. But sometimes agents find creative people off-putting. No matter how strange you might be perceived by an agent, you can never go wrong by being polite, respectful, nice, and professional.

Your agent is not your mom, your best friend, or your therapist. Be friendly and open with them, but keep your emotional problems to yourself. To keep your agent engaged, you need to keep working, be exciting, and show them you're a moving success train they'd be crazy not to jump on. An agent is a professional associate. They make money when you make money, so work hard and do good work.

You can solicit agents. Call any agency and ask who the junior agents are who will accept unsolicited submissions. When you talk to those agents, the first thing they'll want to know is what experience you have. You'll likely be wasting your time unless you have a lot of experience and can send them a sample of your published work.

Another key to getting an agent is living in New York or Los Angeles.

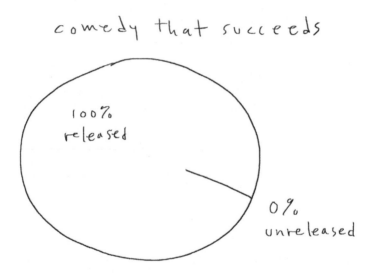

Agents come to improv and stand-up shows in New York and Los Angeles looking for new talent to represent. They don't go to shows in any other cities in the United States. So if you want to be "discovered" by an agent, that's where you need to be. When you live in New York or Los Angeles, people in the industry take you more seriously.

Associate yourself with comedy organizations in New York and Los Angeles, such as the local stand-up scene and the improv scene. Go to entertainment-industry parties. Meet other comedy professionals. You'll meet agents and learn about opportunities.

If an agent likes you, they'll alert you to job openings in the industry and help you get those jobs. Agents may not ask you to sign a contract to represent you—some operate on handshake deals with clients.

If you have an agent, your agent may recommend you also get a manager. And if you have a manager but not an agent, your manager might recommend that you get an agent. Take their advice seriously, but make your own decision. If you just want to get a job as a staff writer on a TV show, you probably only need an agent. Agents can look over contracts and an experienced agent will be just as competent as an entertainment lawyer in finding rough spots in a contract. But if you have grander aspirations and want career guidance, having both a manager and an agent can help propel you. An agent's job is to find you work. A manager's job is to guide your career and find the right kind of work to achieve your goals. If you get work, you might also want an entertainment lawyer. All of these people work on commission. Typically, the agent will take 15 percent, the manager 10, and the lawyer 5.

It's possible to get an agent without moving to New York or Los Angeles, but it rarely happens. The only way to do that is to make the agents come to you, which you can do only by building a successful comedy brand of your own.

BUILDING YOUR OWN BRAND

We've covered the first way to get your work in front of audiences and make money, which is to submit your work to existing brands. Building your own brand is the second. To succeed, you're best served doing both.

Submitting your ideas to other brands can certainly lead to paid work in comedy. Starting your own brand, on the other hand, won't pay much at first. In fact, it will likely cost money. But it's a critical investment in your future.

Building your own brand will make you more attractive to editors, agents, or other people who can offer you paid work. Building your own brand can also lead to actual fans and earnings without the help of established brands. Once you have these things, you're a more attractive prospect for high-paying jobs. If your brand becomes successful, you may not need or want those jobs.

Here are some of the ways you can build your own brand:

A PUBLICATION

Start your own comedy blog or publication. All the publications I listed above were just an idea in someone's head at the beginning. Why can't an idea in your head become a publication? You can start on Wordpress or Tumblr or any number of platforms.

A BOOK

You can collect your short pieces in a book or write a longer work and self-publish it on Amazon.

A YOUTUBE CHANNEL

You can put videos on YouTube: sketches, your stand-up, anything.

A WEBSITE

If you intend to be serious about writing humor, you need to have a personal website. Your simple website should have links to your work (including your YouTube channel, book, and publication), a blog where you publish writing that isn't published anywhere else, a short bio, and contact information. When someone Googles your name, you want them to see you're a serious writer who's ready for professional work.

ON STAGE

Get on stage in your town and do stand-up comedy. There is no better way to hone your comedic voice, test your material, and build confidence. In New York or Los Angeles, you can also put up a one-person show that has a very good chance of attracting agents.

SOCIAL MEDIA

For a time, people with funny and original Twitter feeds were getting offered TV writing jobs. You can do the same. Obviously there's no guarantee of a job offer, but dong a funny social-media feed (best done now on a new, hotter platform than Twitter) can build your brand and introduce people to your work.

A PODCAST

It's easy enough to start recording and uploading a podcast. Apply the same principles you apply to a comedy title or piece to your podcast. Make it a great concept. Make it original. Produce it regularly.

A WEB COMIC

Whether you can draw or not, a web comic is a great way to get people to read your writing, and a great way to build the brand of you. Create a unique look that aligns with your website and your other material, align it thematically with your unique comic voice.

Choose wisely. If you sign up to do a daily comic strip, a weekly podcast, or some other regular product, you'll be on the hook to produce that product for a long time if you want to build a brand. Make sure you want to do it, and make sure people are responding positively. If they aren't, adjust what you're doing until they are.

STREET ART

There are no rules. Get your comedy out into the world however you can. Connor O'Malley not only made his own YouTube videos, he also posted street-art vines and fake reviews of products online. He didn't even have to start his own website or blog. He simply used others, writing hilarious reviews on Yelp or Amazon, always signing them with the same name, and building a reputation for his unique comic voice. These efforts ultimately got him hired as a writer on *Late Night with Seth Myers*.

THE ROAD AHEAD

Quantity is the key to quality not just at the joke level. Yes, it's a good idea to write an enormous quantity of funny ideas in order to ferret out the good ones that are worthy of writing or producing, but it's also a good idea to create or produce an enormous quantity of comedy writing or sketches or stand-up that you present to real audiences in a variety of media. At this even more discerning level, you'll ferret out the best of the best ideas. You'll create the quantity necessary to discover the ideas audiences love, that define your voice, and that make you a success.

More detailed information on how to get your work on all these platforms quickly and inexpensively is beyond the scope of this book, but look for the "Comedy Business School" course from me offered through howtowritefunny.com. In it, I'll drill down on these and related endeavors in great detail. I'll offer step-by-step guides for getting your work seen, breaking through psychological barriers, finding opportunities, and making a living from your comedy.

Comedy writing is a competitive field. If you're possessed of amazing skill, after a time you might be able to make a few submissions and be vaulted straight to the front lines of the entertainment business like Simon Rich.

But it's likely going be a long road, building your own brand, working clubs, submitting articles, and possibly moving to New York or Los Angeles. I hope this book will provide you with the leverage to shave some years off that journey.

But if you love writing comedy, years shouldn't matter to you. Enjoy the ride! Stay positive, do good, consistent work, and make people laugh. Keep doing it and getting better at it until you're so good the world can't ignore you.

CHAPTER 17 ACTION STEP

Repeat.

ACKNOWLEDGMENTS

This book wouldn't exist without the support of those who purchased *How to Write Funny* or took my courses at the "Writing with The Onion" training center at the Second City in Chicago or online. I'm glad the book has helped so many people discover or sharpen their ability to write comedy well.

I'm especially grateful to those who allowed me to show their work in this book, Ben Thompson, Christina Devlin, Wes Marfield, Ricardo Angulo, Matthew Prager, Collin Nissan and his *McSweeney's* editor, Chris Monks, David Calkins, Hugh Kelly, Ian Harris, and David Harnden-Warwick.

Many thanks to Tricia England, Mike Gillis, Jermaine Affonso, Agathe Panaretos, Seth Reiss, Drew Dickerson, Tim Sampson, Steve Etheridge, Geoff Squire, and Maureen Monahan for being a part of my teaching team.

Madeline Schmidt was instrumental in marketing this book, Ian Harris in fueling it, Alan Roberts in copyediting it, and Brooke Washington and Dandelion Benson in celebrating it.

I appreciate Mike McAvoy at *The Onion* and Kelly Leonard, Kerry Sheehan, Matt Hovde, and all the staff at *The Onion* and the Second City for partnering with me to brand the courses based on *How to Write Funny* that made this book possible.

Mike Sacks was kind enough to share his expertise for the last chapter.

Ready to amp up your comedy *even more*?

Take your comedy to the next level with Book 3 of the *How to Write Funny* series:

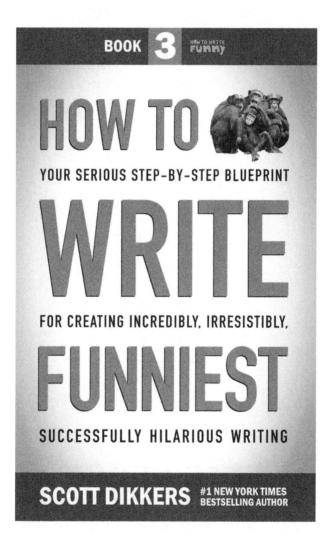

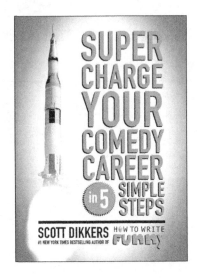